ESSAYS IN ART AND CULTURE

ILLUSTRATION

J. Hillis Miller

Harvard University Press

Cambridge, Massachusetts 1992

For Jessica, Jeremy and Emily

First published in the United States of America in 1992
by Harvard University Press, Cambridge, Massachusetts
Published in Great Britain in 1992 by Reaktion Books, London
Copyright © J. Hillis Miller 1992
All rights reserved
Printed in Great Britain
10 9 8 7 6 5 4 3 2 1

This book is printed on 130gsm Fineblade Smooth,
an acid-free stock made from 100 per cent chemical woodpulp,
and its materials have been chosen for strength
and durability.

Library of Congress Cataloging-in-Publication Data
Miller, J. Hillis (Joseph Hillis), 1928–
Illustration / J. Hillis Miller.
    p.   cm.
ISBN 0-674-44357-8
1. Arts.   2. Deconstruction.   3. Art criticism—History—20th century.
I. Title
NX640.M55   1992
700'.1—dc20   91-28136
                                                     CIP
ISBN 0-674-44357-8

Contents

Acknowledgements   7

Part One   The Work of Cultural Criticism in the Age
of Digital Reproduction   9

Politicizing Art – What are Cultural Studies? –
Benjamin – The Technology of Cultural Studies – The
Thoreau Prototype – The Aporias of Cultural Studies –
Inaugurative Responsibility

Part Two   Word and Image   61

Images et texte – Ruskin – Heidegger – Ruskin on
Holbein – Dickens and Phiz – Turner – Turner's
Doublings – Turner as Second Sun – Goethe – Return
to Turner – *The 'Sun of Venice' Going to Sea* – The Critic
as Illustrator

References   152

List of Illustrations   167

Acknowledgements

I am grateful for the comments and criticisms of those students and colleagues who have listened to parts of this book in oral presentations. Some of these are acknowledged by name in the References. In particular, I thank Ronald Schleifer and Robert Con Davis for inviting me to present a lecture on cultural criticism at a conference at the University of Oklahoma. This ultimately became part One of this book. I thank also Wolfgang Iser for inviting me to present what became part Two of this book in the series of Konstanzer Dialoge at the University of Konstanz. I thank also Max Nänny of the University of Zurich for inviting me to give as a lecture at a conference held there on Word and Image part of the section of this book on Turner. Thomas Dutoit provided an extremely helpful reading of the manuscript. Barbara Cohen, Senior Editor at the University of California at Irvine and my invaluable assistant, did all the hard work of arranging for the illustrations. Without her help the book would have been much delayed. I am grateful to the University of California at Irvine for providing a quarter's leave of absence during which much of this book was completed. The dedication acknowledges the great joys of being a grandfather.

Part One: The Work of Cultural Criticism in the Age of Digital Reproduction

POLITICIZING ART

A Swiss poet, novelist, playwright and critic I know recently attended the Dartmouth School of Criticism and Theory. Since she comes from a country where the study of literature is still more or less centred on literary history and the interpretation of individual works, she was amazed by the relatively little interest the other participants showed in reading literature. They had, however, a deep, wide-ranging and eclectic knowledge of theory. For most of them the centre of literary study has shifted from reading to theory, particularly theory relating literature to history and politics. According to the law that onlookers see most of the game, my friend perceived something that most American academics now take so much for granted as hardly to notice it. The first part of this book will attempt to understand that shift, with particular reference to the rapid burgeoning of cultural studies of various kinds. The second part will explore the relations of picture to word as one practical and theoretical issue important in cultural studies. The issue is important because the objects of cultural studies so often combine visual and verbal materials, for example in film or television, in advertising, in all sorts of illustrated texts. Adeptness in reading pictures as well as words is a skill most cultural critics need. Or rather, what is needed is the ability to read not just pictures and words separately, but the meanings and forces generated by their adjacency, for example in pictures with captions or in illustrated books, newspapers and magazines. Though the relations of picture and word take different forms in different media, at different historical moments, and for different cultural groups, a similar identifiable problematic may persist throughout these differences. My goal in the second part of this book is to identify that.

Walter Benjamin, in a celebrated aphorism at the end of his essay on 'The Work of Art in the Age of Mechanical Reproduction', asserted that if the aestheticization of politics was being brought about by Fascism (*die Ästhetisierung der Politik, welche der Faschismus betreibt*), 'Communism responds by politicizing art' (*Der Kommunismus antwortet ihm mit der Politisierung der Kunst*).[1] The problem with such symmetrical reversals is that they may, in the end, come to the same thing, as Jean-Joseph Goux argues about this particular reversal.[2] To see the state as a work of art is to presume, as the Nazis did, not only that the state is a work of art, the creation of the Führer, but that, as a consequence, art should be in the direct service of the nation-state, the calculated instrument of state ideology. To politicize art, on the other hand, as happened in the Soviet Union, may be to presume that art should be in the direct service of the nation-state, the calculated instrument of state ideology. In both cases art and politics are seen as so intimately related that what happens in one happens in the other. Both tend to presuppose that art is so closely associated with some people or nation-state that it cannot be understood without understanding its roots in a specific language, nation, moment in history, class and gender structure, ideological formation and technological level of production, distribution and consumption.

A little reflection, however, will show that Benjamin's chiasmus is asymmetrical and irreversible. The elements in the two statements not only change places but also change their natures when they are displaced. 'Aestheticization' is not the same thing as 'art'. 'Politicization' is not the same thing as 'politics'. In each case, a tropological transformation replaces a conceptual name. To aestheticize politics is to treat the state as though it were a work of art and therefore to treat human beings as though they were the raw materials of a work of art, able to be manipulated and shaped to fit some rigid scheme, just as dancers are swept into a dance and must obey its pattern, according to a figure used by both Schiller and Yeats. This, says Benjamin, is Fascism. The politicizing of art, on the other hand, the context of Benjamin's essay suggests, means affirming the political value and force of art. Politicizing art means demystifying concepts like genius and eternal value, but also demystifying the idea – present, for example, in Heidegger – that art expresses the essential nature of some nation or race. These are replaced with the assumption that art of a given time is deeply embedded in history,[3] in a particular language and class structure, in specific modes of production, distribution and consumption, particular states of technology, a particular subject-position in the maker. Benjamin attempts to politicize art in this way in his essay. Communism, at least in principle, takes art seriously not just as cultural product but as cultural force.[4]

To 'politicize' art is one project of cultural criticism as it has rapidly developed into a leading way of organizing teaching and research in the United States and in Europe. At the same time, the actual development of twentieth-century art has been toward an internationalization that makes considerations of local provenance perhaps less and less pertinent. This development of international styles in high art has accompanied technological developments that have collaborated in the uprooting of art and popular culture from their local origins. A world-wide culture of blue jeans and tee-shirts, film, television, video-cassettes, popular music on radio and CDs is irreversibly displacing, or at least transforming, local cultures everywhere. The local deeper differences remain, but the surface culture is remarkably the same around the world. The power of this culture to erode local differences is so great that it makes one extremely anxious about the possibility of enhancing or developing those regional specificities that seem the normal and proper human condition. To do so, however, to give those fragile, marginalized ways of living a vital power of self-determination, is one main goal of cultural studies.

One anecdotal example will indicate what I mean. One Sunday a couple of years ago I was in Kathmandu, Nepal, in the house of an extended upper-caste family of Brahmins. This was about as far away from my own, American, culture as I had ever been. How did they spend the Sunday afternoon? By watching on VCR a movie in Hindi. Much can be said about these films. They are the product of a complex indigenous film tradition, but to an American eye they look, in part, something like American films and television shows of urban violence, for example 'L.A. Law' or 'Miami Vice'. The latter is shown on Nepali state television.

A similar uprooting and internationalizing has happened to the university. Rather than being, as was the case in the nineteenth century, in the direct service of a specific nation state and its aspirations, each university is now more and more truly universal, transnational. The university, for

11

example, works in the service of multinational pharmaceutical or computer industries. In the case of the humanities, a given university shares in a collective research and teaching effort that knows few national boundaries and limitations. Young scholars from all over the world attend the Dartmouth School of Criticism and Theory. Moreover, technological developments associated with copying machines, fax machines and computers are transforming the conditions of research and teaching in the humanities, just as mechanical reproduction transformed the conditions of the making and using of art in the nineteenth and early twentieth centuries, as Benjamin argues in 'The Work of Art in the Age of Mechanical Reproduction'. What is the place of cultural studies in this age not of mechanical but of digital reproduction? What are the manifest and latent presuppositions of cultural studies and their place in the university and in society at this moment in history? What do you find, I am asking, if you make culture studies the object of cultural study?

Cultural studies of various sorts are no doubt overdetermined. They have many, and to some degree contradictory, sources, or perhaps it would be better to say concomitant factors, to avoid begging a question that ought to be at the heart of any interrogation of the significance of cultural studies. This is the question of what causes cultural changes. One thing is certain: it would be a gross error to assume that the reorientation from language to history, politics and society as the focal points of humanistic study is merely another shift in the winds of critical fashion. The shift is a response to profound motivations in the multitude of (mostly younger) scholars who now see such studies as their vocation. Among these motivations are ideological ones that may not be readily apparent to those caught up in the changes.

In saying this I am aware that just as persons undergoing psychoanalysis resist having their neuroses identified and brought to light, so all of us resist having our ideological presuppositions identified and brought to light. If ideology is the confusion of linguistic with material reality, it also depends, as Althusser said, on functioning unconsciously, on being unthought out, 'impensée'. To think it out, to reflect theoretically about it, may be to risk disabling it. This is one of the things that is meant when theory is falsely accused of being nihilistic. On the other hand, even if insight and effective action always pivot on an area of blindness necessary to their functioning, that blindness may damage both the insight and the effective action. Such blindness is not necessarily the benign and productive centre of a radiant light. The insight may be no more than another form of disastrous blindness. The action may be effective but have dismayingly different results from those intended. It is probably best to try to see as clearly as possible, even though clear-seeing or theory is always at least one step behind a blindness that always reforms itself and that is the condition of seeing. The term 'ideological' may itself not be appropriate if it is implicitly or explicitly set against the idea of real material conditions, since the latter is itself an ideological concept requiring critical scrutiny.

WHAT ARE CULTURAL STUDIES?

Cultural studies take a number of different institutional forms, forms not entirely congruent with one another either in theory or in practical, political and institutional orientation. Ethnic studies do not have quite the same presuppositions as women's studies, nor are either of those the same as the transformation of what used to be called American studies into a multi-media, multi-linguistic form of cultural studies. Different from all these are 'new historical' studies as applied to Renaissance or Victorian English literature. Still different are British Birmingham School cultural studies, with their strongly institutionalized pedagogical programmes and their particular political agenda within a Britain still governed by the Conservative Party. By comparison, cultural studies in the United States or in Australia (where there is a boom in such studies) are diffuse, heterogeneous and not yet firmly institutionalized.[5] Nevertheless, certain presuppositions tend to persist throughout all these different forms of cultural studies. I shall focus to some degree on minority discourses.

(1) Cultural studies tend to assume that a work of art, popular culture, literature or philosophy can best be understood if accompanied by an attempt to understand the work's historical context, including the political elements of that history: the material, social, class, economic, technological and gender circumstances in which the work was produced and

consumed. If you want to understand Henry James, study the conditions of the publishing industry during the period in which James wrote. These conditions are essential to the meaning of James's work, not adventitious to it. The work, whether of high art or of popular culture, can only be fully understood by way of an understanding of the subject position of the maker, the place in society where the maker stood. 'Subject' here is, of course, a pun. It means both subjectivity and subjected to, or subject to, as when we say 'Queen Victoria's subjects'.

(2) Cultural studies are cross-disciplinary and multi-media in orientation. They presuppose a crossing or breaking down of traditional disciplinary separations. They study films, novels, poems, television soap operas, advertising, painting, popular music, photography, dress and culinary practices side by side as concomitant evidence of a given culture's state at a given time. They use procedures developed in the social sciences as well as in the humanities. Cultural studies owe much to the procedures of anthropology and ethnography, though they are also critical of these disciplines. The interdisciplinarity of cultural studies would appear to put in question in various ways earlier language-oriented theory, for example, its concentration on literary or philosophical texts. Nevertheless, though the focus on popular culture displaces scholarly attention from language to signs of all sorts, a reading of these signs is still necessary. The question is what changes in procedure are involved when we read an advertisement or a soap opera rather than a poem, a novel or a philosophical treatise.

(3) Cultural studies deliberately attempt to break down the assumption that there is an agreed-upon canon of works that ought to be the centre of humanistic studies. Partly, as in ethnic studies and women's studies, this assault on the canon is motivated by the desire to include in the curriculum hitherto neglected works by women and minorities. Partly, as in the new American studies, it is motivated by the presupposition that if your focus is culture, not literature or art according to some assumption that there is a timeless pantheon of classics, then popular culture is as important or even more important than highbrow works produced for an élite of connoisseurs.

(4) Cultural studies tend to assume that a work of art,

popular culture, literature or philosophy not only can best be understood in its historical context, but also has its best value or purchase on the world if it remains understood in relation to some specific and local people, a people defined by language, place, history and tradition, the experience of African–American or Chicano/a people, for example, or those who wrote for the theatre or attended it in Shakespeare's England. This does not mean that a work does not have value when it is transferred to a new context, but that it had best not be detached in that displacement from an understanding of the subject position of its maker. To do so is to be in danger of sentimentalizing or aestheticizing the work. The work, for example, may be uprooted and made into a quaint aesthetic toy for the hegemonic class of consumers, as 'Anglos' may admire reproductions of Chicano/a murals, whereas each cultural artefact is best seen, to borrow phrases from Abdul JanMohamed, as 'a performative utterance/event as opposed to its existence as an aesthetic object'.[6]

Cultural studies do not see the context of a cultural artefact as a passive, stable and timeless background of ethnicity. The work is not just embedded in its context, as a rock is embedded in the earth or a precious stone in a ring. That context is a dynamic, heterogeneous field, constantly changing, in part through the performative effects on it of newly made cultural artefacts. Nor is the ethnic culture safely sequestered from the dominant culture. In an important unpublished paper, in part a response to an earlier version of this book's first part, David Lloyd distinguishes between individual ethnic cultures and minority discourse. An ethnic culture, says Lloyd, 'can be conceived as turned, so to speak, towards its internal differences, complexities and debates, as well as to its own traditions or histories, projects and imaginings'. An ethnic culture

is transformed into a minority culture only along the lines of its confrontation with a dominant state formation which threatens to destroy it by direct violence or by assimilation. Minority discourse is articulated along this line, and at once registers the loss, actual and potential, and offers the means to a critique of dominant culture precisely in terms of its own internal logic.[7]

The context to which a given artefact is related by cultural studies is not a homogeneous ethnic culture, but that culture both as differentiated within itself and as threatened, damaged and displaced by the dominant culture. The situations of Native American and Chicano/a cultures within the United States are good examples of that damage and displacement.[8]

(5) Cultural studies tend to define themselves through a set of oppositions that may appear to be reductively binary: élite versus popular, hegemonic as against marginal, theory as against praxis, cultural artefact as reflection of culture as against art as the maker of culture, and so on. Such thinking has its dangers, as the example of the apparent reversibility of the politicizing of art into the aestheticizing of politics suggests. Some hierarchy and possibility of dialectical sublation tend to be assumed. It is difficult to get thought and practice to move outside the presuppositions that are being contested.

Many cultural critics are fully aware of this problem, both in its theoretical form and as a practical problem, to use one of these oppositions. Abdul JanMohamed, for example, distinguishes between 'binary negation' and 'negation as analogue'. He may be punning on the terms 'analogue' and 'analog', thereby alluding to two different forms of calculation possible in computer systems, binary and analog.[9] Binary negation is dialectical, subject to hierarchical ordering and to the kind of recuperation I have named as a danger. Mystifying presuppositions about grounding origin and pre-existing goal are almost inevitably implied. Negation by analogue sees each element as part of a differential series without hierarchical priority, without fixed original or end.[10] I see this distinction as a crucial theoretical point. It is crucial because cultural studies must hold on to it firmly if they are to resist being recuperated by the thinking of the dominant culture they would contest. It is also a good example of the debt of cultural studies to previous theoretical work developed in other contexts. The distinction is, for example, something like the distinction between two kinds of representation or repetition, repetition as copy and repetition as simulacrum, as developed in different ways by Derrida, Foucault or Deleuze.[11]

(6) Cultural studies have an uneasy relation to theory, particularly to the Deconstructive or Post-Structuralist theory that preceded them and without which they would have been impossible in the form they have taken. On the one hand, cultural studies are theoretical through and through, so much

so that 'critical theory' is almost a synonym for 'cultural studies'. On the other hand, they are sometimes deeply suspicious of theory, sometimes define themselves as resolutely anti-theoretical, and would stress their practical orientation as against the 'sterile' ratiocinations and élite institutional placement of 'pure theory'. The fear is that since theory was developed by the élite dominant culture it cannot be appropriated by cultural studies without disabling the latter in some form of recuperation. David Lloyd, in the unpublished paper cited above, has argued forcefully against this assumption. For Lloyd, theory is an essential part of minority discourse, essential to its practical political goals of changing the university and gaining self-determination for minority individuals and groups.

(7) This uneasy relation to theory goes with an attitude towards reading that is somewhat different from either that of the New Criticism or of so-called Deconstruction. If reading, for Deconstruction, or rhetorical criticism, is the centre of a humanistic study that is oriented towards the understanding of language or other signs and that presupposes some element of the unique and unaccountable in each work, cultural studies may sometimes be primarily thematic, paraphrastic and diagnostic in their way of reading. Just as a physician or psychoanalyst must go rapidly through the details of a physical or psychological illness to diagnose it as a case of measles or of schizophrenia, in order to get on with the urgently needed treatment, so the practitioner of cultural studies sometimes goes as rapidly as possible through the evident features of the work to diagnose it as another case of the particular culture it manifests. The orientation is more toward the culture and less toward the work in itself, even though the heterogeneity of each culture is in principle recognized. Rhetorical reading, or so-called Deconstruction, presupposes that only an active and interventionist reading of texts and other cultural artefacts can be socially and politically effective. A merely thematic reading will remain caught in the ideology that is being contested, whatever its overt theoretical or political assertions. In the realm of words, which are the medium of cultural criticism, only an active reading wrestling with the excess of language or other signs over transparent meaning, a wrestling with what might be called the material dimension of signs, will *work*, that is, effect

changes in the real institutional and social worlds. This is an important point in my argument, to which I shall return.

(8) Cultural studies, finally, are explicitly political. They stress the performative over the merely theoretical in what they do. Their goal is the transformation of the university by realigning present departments and disciplines and establishing new ones. Through the refashioning of the university they want to dismantle the present dominant culture and empower ones that are at present peripheral – minorities, women, gays and lesbians, all those disadvantaged, silenced, without power. This empowering means not just preserving the minority cultures as they are or have been, but giving members of those minority cultures the ability to transform their own cultural forms and to repair the damage done to them by the dominant culture in new self-determined and self-determining creations.

The political aspect of cultural studies is the noblest and most attractive. Who could oppose the righting of injustice and the enfranchising of the disenfranchised? Who would not be attracted by the idea that he or she is not just reading this or that work, but furthering the cause of universal justice? The problem is to know you are really doing that, or at least to know as much as can be known about why you cannot know. Theoretical reflection may be essential to this – or perhaps may keep it from happening. That is the question. Since what cultural studies produce is discourse, whatever effect they have will, properly speaking, be performative, that is, a way of doing things with words. That effect will, therefore, be subject to linguistic constraints on the relation between power and knowledge in discourse.

The overtly political aspect of cultural studies is disquieting from the point of view of the traditional self-definition of the university as the place of disinterested pursuit of knowledge. The modern Western university has defined itself as the place where the principle of reason reigns. Everything can and should be rationalized, its grounding principle identified, and the results of this research stored in the vast archives of what has been made reasonable. That self-definition has no doubt been a blinded cover for the perpetuation of the dominant white, male Eurocentric ideology. The university is not disinterested at all, it is an instrument of power. It is not a matter of politicizing an apolitical university. The university is already political through and through. Nevertheless, the overt definition of a component of the university as oriented toward revolutionary transformation not only of the university but of the society whose instrument the university is, rocks the boat quite a bit. It may be that there has been so little resistance to this assertion of the goal of cultural studies just because those hegemonic custodians of the old university cannot bring themselves to take cultural studies seriously, though that is now beginning to change. Many of those running the university are scientists, secure in the knowledge of their power to remake the world. They are probably wrong in taking the goals of cultural studies so lightly, though the university's powers of recuperation are immense, as proponents of cultural studies recognize.[12]

A further danger is the appropriation of cultural studies by the dominant culture. This is already happening. Cultural critics are, for example, enlisted for the work of the United States Information Service or for the British Council. One cultural critic, for example, was asked recently to provide the British Council with the twenty-five best records by British rock groups for diffusion abroad as examples of the vitality of British culture. The celebration and transformative liberation of cultural diversity by cultural studies can, with dismaying ease, be transformed into a promulgation by the dominant culture of a liberal pluralism that falsifies and covers over the actual power and property relations between the dominant and marginal cultures within a given nation. I shall, later, consider ways of resisting that appropriation.

BENJAMIN

The project of cultural studies is riven by a set of paradoxes, contradictions, or, more properly, aporias. These rhetorical terms are justified by the fact that cultural studies is a way of saying something and doing something (political) with words. After identifying these aporias I shall suggest a way to respond actively to the impasses to which they may lead. The aporias may be approached by way of Benjamin's key terms in 'The Work of Art in the Age of Mechanical Reproduction'.

Benjamin's essay depends on the opposition between the person embedded in a tradition, on the one hand, and the 'masses', on the other. This opposition is symmetrically matched with the opposition between the aura of the unique work of art and the lack of aura in the reproduced work. The term *aura* is one of those remnants of religious or metaphysical thinking that crosses against the grain of Benjamin's commitment to Marxist dialectical materialism. The concept of *reine Sprache*, or pure speech, in Benjamin's essay 'The Task of the Translator' in *Illuminations* is another example. *Aura* is a somewhat covert transformation of words like *Erscheinung* or *Scheinen* used in Benjamin's earlier work, notably in the *Ursprung des deutschen Trauerspiels* (translated as *The Origin of German Tragic Drama*). These words explicitly echo Idealist aesthetics, for example, Hegel's definition of Beauty as 'das sinnliche *Scheinen* der Idee'.[13] Though Benjamin begins 'The Work of Art in the Age of Mechanical Reproduction' with the claim that his theses in the essay 'brush aside a number of outmoded concepts, such as creativity and genius, eternal value and mystery – concepts whose uncontrolled (and at present almost uncontrollable) application would lead to a processing of data in the Fascist sense' (E, 218; G, 149), it is difficult to see how the concept of aura is different from the concepts of eternal value and mystery, unless one can say that the term aura as used by Benjamin is the critique or deconstruction of the idea of mystery.

For traditional men and women the work of art was unique, made once only, impossible to reproduce, except in degraded form, since the copy would lack the authenticity and aura of the original work, so be worthless. The work was placed within the temple, church or other pre-ordained place, where its aura was preserved (illus. 1). Along with its aura went 'the unique appearance [*Erscheinung*] of a distance, however close it may be' (E, 222; G, 154). Aura is a glow bringing into sight a far-off meaning or ground of meaning, but that meaning is brought into sight as distant. As Benjamin says in a footnote:

Distance is the opposite of closeness. The essentially distant object is the unapproachable one. Unapproachability [*Unnahbarkeit*] is indeed a major quality of the cult image. True to its nature, it remains 'distant, however close it may be'. The closeness which one may gain from its material substance does not impair the distance which it retains in its

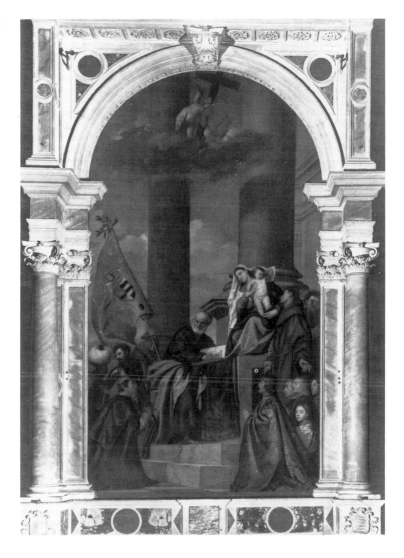

1 Titian, *The Pesaro Madonna*, 1519–26.

appearance [*Erscheinung*]' (E, 243; G, 177; English translation slightly altered).

Even if you touch and handle a cult image, it retains its distance in its shining forth. Here again is that word *Erscheinung*, with its links to Idealist theories of art.

Mass reproduction, on the other hand, brings works from all times and places near to the mass consumer, for example in illustrated magazines and in television shows that bring great masterpieces (and a lot of other things) into our living-rooms. For the masses, the aura of the work of art has disappeared in universal familiarity and closeness.[14] This closeness is not so much physical as psychological, or even, negatively, 'spiritual'. It is the opposite of *Erscheinung*. Such closeness accompanies the possibility of reproducing the work as often as we like in various media of increasing sophistication.[15] The 'cult value' (*Kultwert*) of works of art has been replaced by 'exhibition value' (*Ausstellungswert*). A religious painting may be displayed in a museum where it can be seen by thousands of unbelieving spectators, or it may be used in an advertisement (illus. 2). In a development not mentioned by Benjamin, a work intended for unique display in a museum or home, in an aestheticized corruption of aura, may be reproduced in an advertisement. Religious or aesthetic works may also be duplicated in forms increasingly far from the original, for example by scanner for digital storage and retrieval.

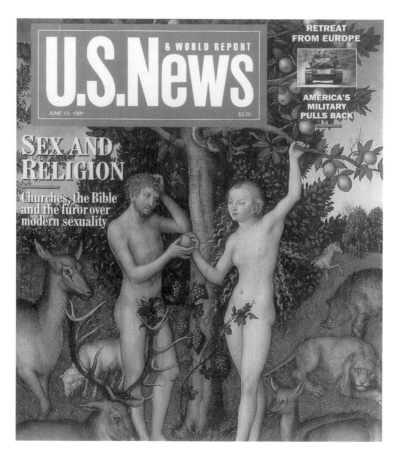

2 Lucas Cranach, *Adam and Eve*, cover of *U.S. News & World Report* magazine.

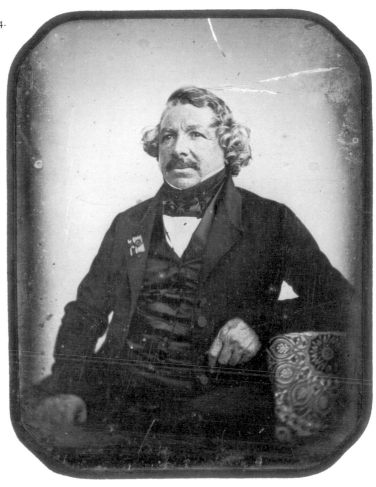

More is at stake, however, in the opposition between
Kultwert and *Ausstellungswert*, as a look at the local linguistic
grain of section Six of 'The Work of Art' (E, 225–6; G, 157–8),
will show. Having said that photography is the form of mechanical reproduction in which exhibition value begins to displace cult value (though, of course, at first photographs were
not markedly easier to reproduce than other forms of mechanical reproduction, like the printed engraving), Benjamin, in a
striking passage, goes on to argue that cult value still remains
in early portrait photographs:

> It is no accident that the portrait was the focal point of
> early photography. The cult of remembrance of loved ones,
> absent or dead, offers a last refuge for the cult value of the

picture. For the last time the aura emanates from the early photographs in the fleeting expression of a human face. This is what constitutes their melancholy, incomparable beauty.

The melancholy beauty of early portrait photographs (see illus. 3) is not to be compared to anything else, because such photographs express a double loss.

On the one hand, they are the product of prosopopoeia, traditionally defined as the ascription of a name, a face or a voice to the absent, the inanimate or the dead. Benjamin's phrasing echoes part of that definition word for word. Portrait photographs bring near in their distance 'loved ones, absent or dead'. The aura that emanates from such photographs arises from the way those who remember through them the absent or dead project a life into the human image on the inanimate coated paper, a life it does not actually have. The absent are present in their absence. This generates the melancholy beauty of the cult of remembrance as sustained by portrait photographs. The words 'melancholy' and 'beauty' here tie Benjamin's thought not only to *The Origin of German Tragic Drama* but also to the definition by Hegel of Beauty as the sensible appearance of the Idea. Aura cannot be separated from Beauty (*Schönheit*). *Beauty* here is a technical word referring to eighteenth- and nineteenth-century aesthetic theory.

On the other hand, portrait photographs are not just melancholy because they connect beauty to loss. They have an 'incomparable' melancholy because they mark the historical moment when cult value was disappearing for good. Photography caused a historical crisis or turning-point in which cult value vanished forever, to be replaced by exhibition value and mechanical reproduction.

This happened as photographs came no longer to be used as mediating images of the absent or dead. Photographs of urban scenes began to be made from which human faces and figures were altogether absent, as if prosopopoeia no longer was able to keep them there:

But as man withdraws from the photographic image, the exhibition value for the first time shows its superiority to the ritual value.

Benjamin's example of this is photographs made by Atget

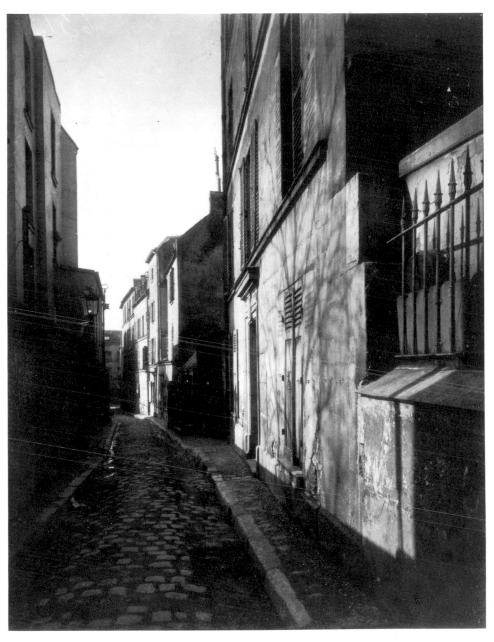

4 Eugène Atget, *Rue Saint-Rutique*, March 1922.

around 1900 of deserted Paris streets (illus. 4). The photographs by Charles Langdon Coburn used as illustrations for the 'New York' edition (1907–9) of Henry James's works would be another example, to be discussed later. Atget photographed empty Paris streets, says Benjamin, as if they were scenes of a crime. What crime is that? It must be the social crime committed or suffered by people who are now not only absent or dead but who are no longer able to be remembered through portrait photographs with their aura of a distant presence. Just as the scene of a crime is photographed for the purpose of establishing evidence, so Atget's photographs are evidence of a different kind. In this case the evidence is historical. Photographs become, as they certainly are for us today, 'standard evidence for historical occurrences, and they acquire a hidden political significance'. The significance is 'hidden' presumably because it is not spelt out in so many words, but must be read from the photograph as evidence of what man has done to man.

An example from our own day, though not one from which human figures are lacking, is the recent presentation on American Public Television of a series called 'Making Sense of the Sixties'. This was being shown at the very moment that the United States plunged itself into a war in the Middle East not entirely unlike the Vietnam War, though of course there are differences, for example in the character of the 'enemy', as well as in the rapidity of the Allies' disengagement from the Gulf War. The Sixties have been abundantly recorded in photographs and films. The historical evidence is waiting there to be understood. The difference between our film records of the Sixties and Atget's photographs of empty streets is that human figures and faces have now become impersonal items among others in the repertory of available historical evidence. This is just what Benjamin says happened to film actors, as opposed to the aura of personal presence still there in the actor on the stage (E, 229; G, 161–2). He cites a passage of 1932 from Rudolf Arnheim describing how in film the actor is 'a stage prop characteristically chosen . . . inserted at the proper place' (E, 230, altered; G, 162).

Having said that photographs empty of human figures have become standard historical evidence, Benjamin concludes section Six of 'The Work of Art' with a problematic distinction that will help me establish the terms for my investigation of the relation of picture and word in part Two of this book, for example in Victorian illustrated novels. Those photographs by Atget, says Benjamin, 'demand a specific kind of approach; free-floating contemplation is not appropriate to them'. 'Free-floating contemplation' presumably is the approach appropriate to works with cult value and aura, for example a painting of a madonna in a church or a portrait photograph on the mantelpiece of one's dead great-great-grandmother. Atget's photographs are another matter: 'They disturb the viewer [*Sie beunruhigen den Betrachter*]. He feels he must seek a determined, settled, or appointed way to them [*Er fühlt: zu ihnen muß er einen bestimmten Weg suchen*]' (E, 226; G, 158). (Zohn's English translation here – 'They stir the viewer; he feels challenged by them in a new way' – is incorrect.)

For Benjamin, the predetermined way to reach such photographs can only be given by words, by captions in the case of photographs in illustrated magazines or in silent films. Now picture cannot be understood without accompanying word, whereas the title on a painting from the age of aura had 'an altogether different character'. Benjamin apparently means that the title of a painting is not at all necessary to our contemplative approach to the painting. Captions, on the other hand, are necessary 'signposts' (*Wegweiser*) that determine for the viewer the way to approach a modern photograph or a silent film. Can we believe that the relation between picture and word changed in this way when the photograph was invented? On the face of it, this seems an extremely dubious idea.

The final sentence of Benjamin's development of this in section Six seems not wholly coherent. It suggests two contradictory determinants of the meaning of a single frame in a cinematic sequence. 'The directives which the captions give to those looking at pictures in illustrated magazines', says Benjamin, 'soon become even more explicit and more imperative in the film where the interpretation of each single picture appears to be prescribed by the sequence of all preceding ones' (translation slightly altered). If the interpretation of each single picture appears to be written ahead of time (*vorgeschrieben*) by the sequence of preceding pictures, why is a caption (*Beschriftung*: a word related, of course, to *vorgeschrieben*) necessary? It must be because without the signpost of a caption even the control over interpretation of the sequences of frames in cinema is not enough to orient the onlooker and show him the way to go. In the age of aura the picture spoke for itself. Now words must speak for it, or the viewer is lost (illus. 5). As I shall show, Mark Twain had an opinion about that.

Benjamin's hierarchically arranged oppositions support a familiar but now somewhat discredited historical narrative: once upon a time there was aura, cult, tradition, possessed only by those within the culture. Now there is exhibition, film, popular media catering to the masses and keeping them in a state of mystification. Their real material and ideological conditions of life are hidden from them by the mass media. The media mediate delusions, delusions often uncritically shared by the makers of mass-culture products. To say that this historical narrative is now somewhat discredited is an important point in my argument. Much is at stake in the persistence in the project of cultural studies, in the ambitious proposal for computer-based research in the humanities described below, or even in so sophisticated a thinker as Benjamin, of one form or another of the genetic paradigm. This model of thought allows literary or cultural history to be retold as a unified story, a story with identifiable beginning, predetermined goal, and organic, causal or dialectical continuity along the way. This paradigm has been persuasively challenged in its Hegelian form by Marx, though reaffirmed in a new form in dialectical materialism. The genetic paradigm has been challenged more generally by Nietzsche, and then put in question again by so-called Deconstruction, for example in the reading of Nietzsche's *The Birth of Tragedy* in Paul de Man's 'Genesis and Genealogy'.[16] To say that a cultural artefact is rooted in the culture from which it arises and can only be understood or remain effective in that context, or to say that big computer databases will allow understanding of the genesis of a work like Thoreau's *Walden*, is to yield to the attraction of one form or another of the genetic thinking that remains an almost irresistible trap for thought. My own essay here may be at first mistakenly understood as arguing that technological changes are irresistibly causing changes in scholarship and in the university.

The example in Benjamin's essay of such a historical story is the changes wrought by the invention of photography and

5 F.W. Murnau, *Sunrise*, 1927, still from silent film with intertext.

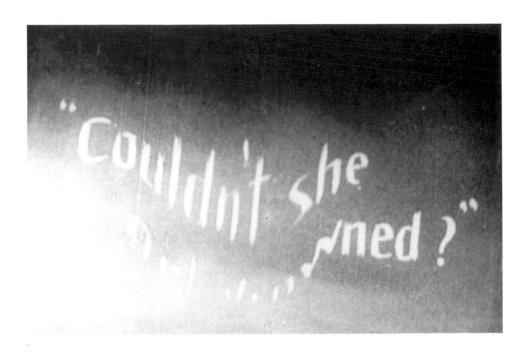

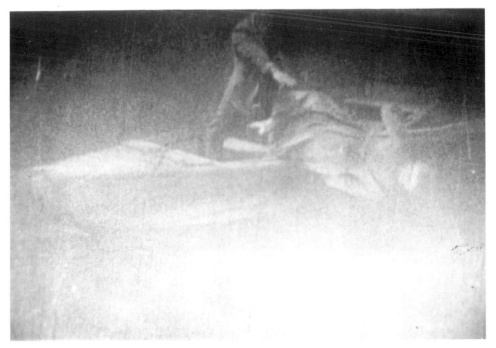

then of moving pictures. His essay is one of the first important reflections on the significance of cinema. The basic presupposition of Benjamin's essay is a Marxist dialectical material one. Technological changes, the invention of the photograph, then silent film, and then 'talkies', have irreversibly transformed both artworks in themselves and everyone's relation to art. These changes include works of the past made in the age of aura, cult and tradition. Though Benjamin allows that films can 'promote revolutionary criticism of social conditions, even of the distribution of property', he asserts that 'as a rule no other revolutionary merit can be accredited to today's film than the promotion of a revolutionary criticism of traditional concepts of art' (E, 231; G, 163).

Benjamin's focus is on the sweeping changes that the material and technological aspects of film production are making both in society and in our sense of art: 'Mechanical reproduction of art changes the reaction of the masses toward art' (E, 234). It is difficult to see how, on Benjamin's terms, film of any sort can do other than reinforce the social changes that the technique of film causes, whatever the thematic content of the film. Benjamin's observations about film anticipate Michel Foucault's insights into the policing power of technology. Foucault speaks of 'new procedures of power, which operate not by right but by technique, not by law but by normalization, not by punishment but by control, which are exercised on levels and forms which exceed the state and its apparatuses'.[17] The opposition between revolutionary film and film consciously promoting bourgeois illusions breaks down before Benjamin's powerful argument for the determining force of film technique as the most advanced means of technical reproduction in his day.

The problem with all Benjamin's oppositions is that they tend to dissolve through the effort of thinking they facilitate. The person of tradition for whom works of art had an aura is seen to have been in a state of illusion, since the mechanical reproduction of the work deprives it of its aura. If the aura had been really there, no amount of degraded reproduction would have touched that radiance from another world. The fact that the modern work of art is reproducible casts its shadow back not just to remove the aura from traditional works but to reveal that the aura was always an ideological formation. That is what Benjamin means by saying film in itself, as a means of mechanical reproduction, is revolutionary criticism of traditional concepts of art. As the technological changes Benjamin describes have proceeded apace, the opposition between traditional man or woman and the masses disappears, and with it the pertinence of the idea of a people with a specific culture. We are all, to some degree, members of what Benjamin invidiously calls the 'masses'. We are members of a transnational, multilinguistic, worldwide technological culture that makes the pieties of nationalism seem more and more outdated, nostalgic, perhaps even dangerously reactionary.

THE TECHNOLOGY OF CULTURAL STUDIES

The contradictions in the project of cultural studies echo those in Benjamin's essay, but at a later time in world history and technological development. Benjamin writes 'The Work of Art' as though the material working conditions of the scholar and critic were not much changed from what they were in the nineteenth century, or even in the Renaissance. His model appears still to be the scholar working in solitude primarily with books. Such a scholar composes with pen, or on the typewriter, manuscripts not all that different from a Renaissance treatise. These manuscripts are written for an élite audience of intellectuals. Benjamin's ideal of scholarship, one might think, is still apparently the codex book or the essay, the latter not greatly changed since Montaigne. He does not much reflect, at least in 'The Work of Art', on the way the technological changes he describes might be changing his own ways of production. Benjamin, as is well known, was a great book collector. One sometimes adduced, but not wholly persuasive, motive for his suicide is his despair at having to leave his books behind in Paris when he fled the Nazis in 1940. *The Origin of German Tragic Drama* is not a book for popular consumption. Its model is the learned dissertation. One of the features of *The Origin* is the way Renaissance, Romantic and modern scholars are quoted side by side as if they existed in a timeless archive of knowledge. The new scholar adds his work to the archive by recapitulating all that has been written on a given topic and then adding something to it.

Nevertheless, *The Origin* notoriously explodes the genre of the dissertation from within. Benjamin once described the usual academic book as 'an outdated mediation between two different filing systems'. He went on to say that he would like to write a book that consisted entirely of citations. Benjamin proposed a way of writing that would be like a spatial design of juxtaposed patterns, a mosaic, rather than a consecutive argument. Such writing puts side by side fragmentary quotations and other details from many contexts. He called these 'close-ups'.[18] The use of a term from cinema and photography suggests the influence of film on Benjamin's own procedures as a writer. Though the fact is not explicitly signalled in the text of 'The Work of Art', the essay is made up of a series of short, and to some degree discontinuous, numbered sections set side by side in montage. Such techniques also anticipate effects now easily obtainable in hyperbolic complexity on the computer, in confirmation of another of Benjamin's theses in 'The Work of Art', to be discussed below.[19]

Since Benjamin's time, conditions of scholarship in the humanities have radically changed. This has happened in part through social changes that have expanded the traditional disciplines, admitted some women and minorities into the academy, and made the university at least somewhat more democratic. In addition, technological changes are transforming scholarship in the humanities. These changes are parallel to changes in the artwork caused by the development of cinema. At the same time, during the sixty years since Benjamin's essay appeared, technological changes in the mechanical reproduction of the artwork have also rapidly proliferated. After sound-film has come television, then stereos, cassettes, CDS and VCRS, all the familiar paraphernalia of our present way of life, in a rapid acceleration of the cultural changes wrought by film. These changes in the media of art have also conspicuously changed the scholarship and criticism that account for art.

One of Benjamin's most challenging theses in 'The Work of Art in the Age of Mechanical Reproduction' is that 'one of the foremost tasks of art has always been the creation of a demand which could be fully satisfied only later'. He goes on to say that 'the history of every art form shows critical epochs in which a certain art form aspires to effects which could be fully obtained only with a changed technical standard, that

6 *Saga of the Swamp Thing*, © 1983, 1984 and 1987 DC Comics Inc.

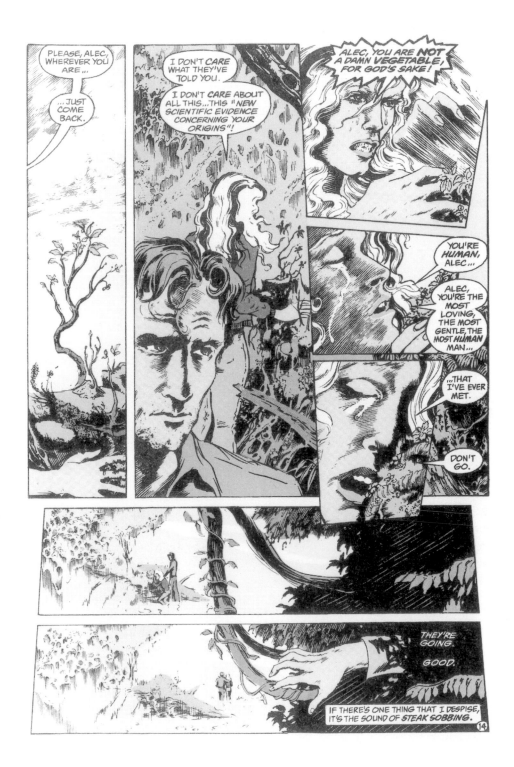

is to say, in a new art form' (E, 237; G, 170). His example is the way Dada in painting and poetry strove with great effort for effects of dissolution and unheard-of creation that could in a short time be much more easily and spectacularly created in film. An example from our contemporary world is those sophisticated new comic books that produce in book form effects borrowed from graphic manipulations, for example superimposed windows, much easier to obtain on a computer, though no doubt the comic books also influenced the computer technology (illus. 6). An example from scholarship is Derrida's *Glas*. This book was not written on the computer, but its format anticipates procedures that are now easy to obtain on a computer. These procedures include the use of different fonts and type sizes, the juxtaposition of parallel columns to make a dialogical text (in the literal sense of 'subject to a double logos'), the use of inserted sidebars or *jalousies* that add more text to the basic doubling (illus. 7). The works of Hegel, Genet and others cited in *Glas* presuppose the large library of references that have been identified and assembled in *Glassary*.[20] They would be much more useful in a hypertext linked textbase on CD-ROM, where the whole context of an allusion could be recovered, the iceberg of which a phrase in *Glas* is just the tip.

Derrida's *The Truth in Painting*, to give another example, uses illustrations and framing 'traits' on the page in a way that produces a multi-media text. The section of this book entitled 'Restitutions' is a 'polylogue' in which an indeterminate number of unidentifiable people of indeterminate sex take turns talking, just as is the case with computer conferencing. In the latter, a single text may be composed by a large group of people who do not know one another in the traditional sense of the face-to-face encounter of two self-enclosed subjects. As Mark Poster has argued, a new form of the dispersal and decentring of the subject is one effect of the computer revolution. The subject has always been subject to signs, produced by reading – decentred, made and remade by signs – but digitized signs will do this in new ways. Here too Derrida has anticipated changes that electronic wrapping will effect in the way we are constituted by signs.[21] Derrida has not just written abstractly about the end of the book. He has produced non-book books that anticipate effects soon to be much more easily obtainable on the computer, just as

Deux passages très déterminés, partiels, particuliers, deux exemples. Mais de l'essence l'exemple se joue peut-être.

Premier passage : la religion des fleurs. Dans la *Phénoménologie de l'esprit*, le développement de la religion naturelle a comme toujours la forme d'un syllogisme : le moment médiat, « la plante et l'animal », comporte une religion des fleurs. Celle-ci n'est pas même un moment, une station. Elle s'épuise presque dans un passage *(Übergehen)*, un mouvement évanouissant, l'effluve flottant au-dessus d'une procession, la marche de l'innocence à la culpabilité. La religion des fleurs serait innocente, la religion des animaux coupable. La religion des fleurs (l'exemple factuel en viendrait d'Afrique, mais surtout de l'Inde) ne reste pas, ou à peine, elle procède à sa propre mise en culpabilité, à sa propre animalisation, comporte une coupable et donc sérieux de l'innocence. Et cela dans la mesure où le même, le soi-même *(Selbst)* n'y a pas encore lieu, ne se donne, encore, que (dans) sa représentation *(Vorstellung)*. « L'inno-

« Die Unschuld der Blumenreligion, die nur selbstlose Vorstellung des Selbsts ist, geht in den Ernst des kämpfenden Lebens, in die Schuld der *Tierreligion*, die Ruhe und Ohnmacht der anschauenden Individualität in das zerstörende Fürsichsein über. »

cence de la *religion des fleurs*, qui est seulement représentation de soi-même sans le soi-même, passe dans le sérieux de la vie agonistique, dans

la culpabilité de la *religion des animaux*; la quiétude et l'impuissance de l'individualité contemplative passe dans l'être-pour-soi destructeur. »

toujours regarder de côté vers l'Inde pour suivre ce passage énigmatique, qui passe très mal, entre l'Extrême-Occident et l'Extrême-Orient. L'Inde, ni l'Europe ni la Chine. Sorte de goulot d'étranglement historique. Resserré comme Gibraltar, « roc stérile et dispendieux », colonnes d'Hercule dont l'histoire appartient à celle de la route des Indes. En ce détroit un peu louche, le panorama est-ouest-eurafrique se rétrécit infiniment. Point de devenir. La pointe rocheuse a souvent changé de nom, néanmoins. Le promontoire s'est appelé Mons Calpe, Notre-Dame-du-Roc, Djebel Tarik (Gibraltar)

qui se dressait alors en l'air, « presque aussi grand que le reste du corps ». A l'origine, donc, les colonnes phalliques de l'Inde, énormes formations, piliers, tours, plus larges

Deuxième passage: la colonne phallique de l'Inde. L'*Esthétique* en décrit la forme au chapitre de l'*Architecture indépendante ou symbolique*. Elle se serait propagée vers la Phrygie, la Syrie, la Grèce où, au cours des fêtes dionysiaques, selon Hérodote cité par Hegel, les femmes tiraient le fil d'un phallus

L'autre — laisse tomber le reste. Risquant de revenir au même. Tombe — deux fois les colonnes, les trombes — reste.

Peut-être le cas *(Fall)* du seing.

Si *Fall* marque le cas, la chute, la décadence, la faillite ou la fente, *Falle* égale piège, trappe, collet, la machine à vous prendre par le cou.

Le seing tombe.

Le reste est indicible, ou presque : non par approximation empirique mais à la rigueur indécidable.

« *Catachrèse*, s.f. 1. Trope par lequel un mot détourné de son sens propre est accepté dans le langage commun pour désigner une autre chose qui a quelque analogie avec l'objet qu'il exprimait d'abord; par exemple, une langue, parce que la langue est le principal organe de la parole articulée; une glace [...] une feuille de papier [...]. C'est aussi par catachrèse qu'on dit : ferré d'argent; aller à cheval sur un bâton. [...] 2. Terme de musique. Dissonance dure et inusitée. E. Κατάχρησις, abus, de κατά, contre, et χρῆσις, usage.

Catafalque, s.m. Estrade élevée, par honneur, au milieu d'une église, pour recevoir le cercueil ou la représentation d'un mort [...] E. Ital. *catafalco*; bas-lat. *catafoltus*, *cadafaldus*, *cadaffalle*, *cadapallus*, *cadapphallus*, *chafallus*. *Cata* est selon Du Cange le bas-latin *catus*, machine de guerre appelée *chat* d'après l'animal; et selon Diez *catare*, voir, regarder; du reste, finalement, ces deux étymologies se confondent, vu que *catus*, chat, et *catare*, regarder, ont le même radical. Reste *falco*, qui, vu les variantes du bas-latin où le *p* se montre, ne peut être que le mot germanique *balk* (voy. **balcon**). *Catafalque* est le même mot que *échafaud* (voy. ce mot).

Cataglottisme, s.m. Terme de littérature ancienne. Emploi de mots recherchés. E. Κατα γλωττισμός, de κατά, indiquant recherche, et γλῶσσα, mot, langue (voy. **glose**). » Littré.
Les ALC sonnent, claquent, éclatent, se réfléchissent et se retournent dans tous les sens, comptent et se décomptent, ouvrant — ici — dans la pierre de chaque colonne des sortes de judas incrustés, créneaux, jalousies, meurtrières pour voir à ne pas se laisser emprisonner dans le colosse, tatouages dans la peau plissée d'un corps

7 Jacques Derrida, page from *Glas*, 1984.

Benjamin did in his use of a mosaic of details juxtaposed in montage without full specification of the logical links between them.

In a similar way, the project of cultural criticism anticipates scholarly procedures that are not quite yet technologically feasible. Cultural studies are one of the concomitants of the technological changes I have been discussing. These technological changes are manifold, but all are replacing mechanical reproduction by digital reproduction. They build on changes in scholarship already effected by the tape-recorder and the photocopying machine, but the primary instrument of the new technology of scholarly reproduction is the personal computer. It is natural to resist Benjamin's thesis that an apparently peripheral technological change like the development of sound-film could transform our perception of

35

objective reality, including even the way we see and value works of art from the past, our perception of a work by Ghirlandaio, for example, or one by Rembrandt. It is also natural to resist the idea that such mechanical changes could redesign all the structures and values of society. In the same way we resist the suggestion that a technological tool like the computer could change the conditions and results of scholarship. How could a technical device modulate our representations of both past and present cultural forms, make us read Shakespeare, Thoreau or Toni Morrison differently?

It would be a grave error, however, to think of the computer as no more than a glorified typewriter. As personal computers become more and more powerful and as more and more programmes and peripherals are added to them, they are becoming a scholar's tool of extraordinary range and power. The new computer world is a realm of multi-media digital reproduction. Pictures, music and words are all treated the same way by the computer. All can be stored in the same file. This file can hardly any longer be called a text, because it is as much to be seen and heard as to be read. Papers (but they are not really papers) written in the new medium will be able to reproduce photographs, film and video clips, paintings, music, sound-tracks and any other material that can be digitized. Electronic mail and networking mean that the individual scholar is in constant connection with other scholars in the same field. What he or she writes may be immediately read, commented on, responded to, altered, added to, or even erased, at least on the target computer. Such scholarship is the product of collaborative research in a new sense, since the researchers working together may be thousands of miles apart. In this new environment of digital reproduction the linear codex book is being replaced by what Richard Lanham calls the 'electronic book'.[22] The electronic book is a multi-media production. It is interactive. The one who uses it may change it. It is, therefore, both unfixed and the product of multiple authorship. It is immaterial, in the sense that it does not exist as fixed hard copy. It has its material base rather in the invisible arrangement of electrons on the disc where it is stored. Copyright laws developed for the printed book do not apply at all easily to the electronic book. A computer network is the material embodiment of a telepathic realm that has always been implicit in the act of

36

reading but that will take new and hyperbolic forms in the computer age. Participation by way of the computer terminal breaks down the borders of each individual consciousness and puts it within a transindividual system of signs. Various forms of telecommunication facilitate the invasion of each separate consciousness by signs that no longer belong to anyone in particular, but are the medium of collective or 'polylogical' thought.[23] However much we have accommodated ourselves to the idea that the fixed self is an ideological illusion, it is an illusion so thoroughly embedded in our social practice that a strong uneasiness is generated, at least in 'me', by the notion that the computer is going to do my thinking for me, or that a vast sea of anonymous digitized thoughts is going to think itself through me by way of the computer.

THE THOREAU PROTOTYPE

A prototypical exploitation of these new possibilities is the Thoreau project being developed by Donald Ross and Austin Meredith at the University of Minnesota.[24] This will be initially for use on the NEXT computer, but will be adapted for other computers. The project will produce a large textbase on CD-ROM bringing together visual, textual and audio materials for the study of Henry David Thoreau. This project will make available a variorum edition of Thoreau's works, not just variant readings at the bottom of the page, but all the editions and manuscripts, superimposed in windows. Along with this will go a large collection of historical materials, graphic, auditory and alphabetic, for example bird-songs and pictures of the birds Thoreau mentions, as well as much of the important secondary work on this writer.[25] All these materials together will make up a 'scholar's workstation' for advanced research on Thoreau. The scholar who uses it will add to it. Updated versions of the CD-ROM holding the materials will periodically be sent to all subscribers (illus. 8).

This facilitation of advanced research by computer technology makes the Thoreau project quite different from computer programmes and databases for undergraduate instruction in literature and art history. A database for advanced research is more specialized, and the links and tracks through it are less predetermined than is the case with a teaching programme. An example of the latter is one aspect

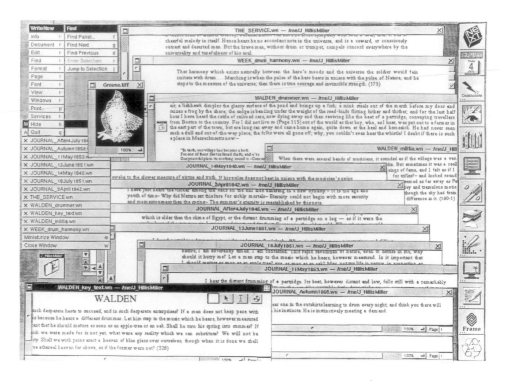

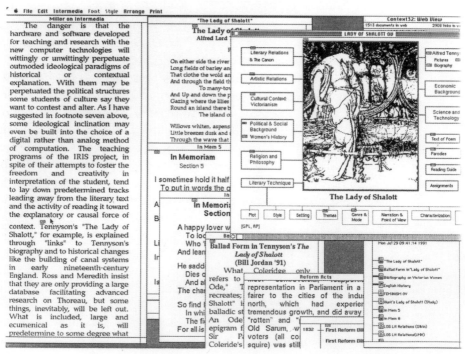

8 Donald Ross,
The Thoreau
Workstation
Project, 1991.

9 George
Landow, IRIS
Project:
Tennyson's 'The
Lady of Shalott',
1991.

of the IRIS project at Brown University (illus. 9).[26] These two ways of using the computer for instruction and for research in the humanities seem likely to proliferate rapidly during the next decade as more and more powerful computers are made available at prices that put them within reach of the student and scholar, even of private scholars outside the university. Such workstations will differ radically from the library of books side by side on the shelves. The scholar will be able to move at will from one region of the textbase to another, executing sophisticated search commands that will allow the instant juxtaposition of pictures, sounds and texts widely separated in origin. Someone working at an obscure junior college anywhere in the country will have at his or her fingertips the equivalent of the Widener Library and the British Library combined. Everything in such databases will be on exactly the same level of availability and importance. From the point of view of the old-fashioned scholar of canonical texts, the élite work of literature, music or art will seem to melt into an indefinitely large context that will be on the same plane of digital availability.

The electronic book will be potentially democratic and anti-canonical not because of some ideologically motivated decision, but by virtue of its technological nature. Such databases will allow a portrait of the complex grain or texture of a historical moment in a particular culture that would not have been available to the people living in that culture. Such reconstruction will recreate past history or make history. This has always been done by historians, but it will be much more evident now, partly because the reconstructions will be infinitely variable, depending on how the textbase is used in a particular case. History will much more evidently not be something objectively out there then, but something constituted now for some particular purpose, in a transformative act of memory oriented toward the future. In this, the digital book will demonstrate in a hyperbolic form another of Benjamin's theses in 'The Work of Art', namely that new technological devices, film in the case he discusses, allow a view of nature and society in no way possible without the aid of the device in question. For film it is the possibility of close-ups, slow motion, montage and other forms of interruption and juxtaposition. For cultural studies the multi-media textbase will put at the computer-user's command possibilities of assemblage and juxtaposition allowing the writing of new histories, histories that never happened as such but that are created on the computer.

The danger is that the hardware and software developed for teaching and research with the new computer technologies will wittingly or unwittingly perpetuate outmoded ideological paradigms of historical or contextual explanation. With them may be perpetuated the political structures some students of culture want to contest and alter. As I have suggested (see reference 9), some ideological inclination may even be built into the choice of a digital rather than analog method of computation. The teaching programmes of the IRIS project, in spite of their attempts to foster the freedom and creativity in interpretation of the student, tend to lay down predetermined tracks leading away from the literary text and the activity of reading it toward the explanatory or causal force of context. Tennyson's 'The Lady of Shalott', for example, is explained through 'links' to Tennyson's biography and to historical changes like the building of canal systems in early nineteenth-century Britain. Ross and Meredith insist that they are only providing a large database facilitating advanced research on Thoreau, but some things, inevitably, will be left out. What is included, large and ecumenical as it is, will predetermine to some degree what can be done with it. The database will presuppose, for example, that it is helpful in understanding *Walden* or *A Week on the Concord and Merrimack Rivers* to hear the songs and see annotated pictures of the birds Thoreau mentions there. That would depend, of course, on the critic's interpretative goals.

The rhetoric of Ross and Meredith's description of their project embodies a set of assumptions about the way scholars do work and ought to work. The key words here are 'associative', 'linked', 'hierarchical', 'dynamic', 'visual' and 'genetic'. 'The system's software', say Ross and Meredith, 'will connect these materials the way scholars do, by association' (p. 3). What, exactly, does that mean? What kind of association is meant? 'Free association', as when we say 'this reminds me of that', and build a whole interpretation on that, perhaps accidental, trick of the mind? Association by analogy or by contingency, that is, by metaphor or by metonymy? It would make a lot of difference which. The question of the kind of explanatory connection set up by these 'links' (p. 3) is left open, though it is the thing most in need of interrogation. The word 'link' implies that the connections are not just associative, but iron-bound and determining, like the links of a chain. Unless you know about canals you will not be able to understand 'The Lady of Shalott'. Unless you know those bird-songs you will not be able to understand Thoreau. Ross and Meredith, as well as the scholars at Brown, emphasize the freedom of the scholar or student to 'browse'. Anyone can use the material freely and move around within it on paths that have not been beaten out beforehand. Nevertheless, the terminology Ross and Meredith use suggests a strong reinforcement of certain paths and a strong presumption of certain forms of explanation. At least this is true in the initial release of the textbase, though one important feature of the project is the way each user can set up his or her own system and adapt the technology to differing theoretical presuppositions.

The software will establish, say Ross and Meredith, three kinds of 'hierarchical' structures among the texts. One is a 'dynamic variorum' (p. 3) superimposing all the successive drafts, including notebook entries and letters, of *Walden* and *A Week*. It is dynamic, presumably, because it is not fixed, because it can be freely manipulated and traversed. Another hierarchy is called 'Thoreau's Study'. It will 'develop a chronological account of all the primary materials' (p. 5). The third is called 'Primary-Secondary Text Links' (p. 6). It will gather a large body of secondary materials, and allow the scholar to retrieve all the relevant passages by 'clicking' on any one passage in Thoreau. Added to these, finally, will be a sophisticated 'Boolean search engine' for retrieving all the passages anywhere in the database that combine a given set of semantic features, 'specified words or phrases' (p. 6).

Each of Ross and Meredith's hierarchies tends to presuppose a mode of explanation that is suggested by their use of the word 'genetic' (p. 4). *Post hoc propter hoc*. What comes earlier determines and explains what comes later. I have written above about the problematic force of the genetic paradigm and the need to put it in question. Ross and Meredith have not fully done this, in spite of their sophisticated allusions to Benjamin and Nietzsche. Three initial ways to understand *Walden*, they suggest, is to make your way through the successive drafts, or to reconstruct the detailed chronology of

Thoreau's reading, writing and other activities that led up to the composition of a certain passage, or to recapitulate all the previous scholarship on a given passage and go on from there. These three hierarchies reflect the way previous scholars assumed the validity of what are, to say the least, conservative or 'old historical' procedures in scholarship. The question is whether these presuppositions are built into the hardware and software, or whether, as Ross and Meredith hope, their textbase can also be used for more innovative forms of research and interpretation. One might fear, for example, that the Boolean search engine presupposes the links from one text to another are literal semantic echoes of the same word or phrase rather than rhetorical or figurative connections. Machine translation has, on occasion, been wrecked on the reef of the same problem, as in the notorious case in which 'The spirit is willing but the flesh is weak' was translated into Russian to mean 'The vodka is good but the meat is rotten'. Ross and Meredith attempt to get around this limitation of computer search programmes by having a more or less elaborate system of keywords attached to each document and each passage so that, for example, Thoreau's phrase 'a different drummer' might lead the scholar to the mating-call of the prairie chicken rather than just to literalized military associations.

Ross and Meredith's stress, finally, on the superiority of visual laying-out of material over the making of verbal connections through reading tends to minimize the activity of reading and suggests the explanatory force of spatial juxtaposition: 'The scholar will see Clapper's genetic text [of *Walden*] then, but in a more usable, visual form than has ever before been contemplated' (p.4). The hard work of reading the primary text tends to disappear in the spatial web of associations, with their implicit explanatory force, the new technology will make it possible to create with graphic interfaces and superimposed windows. It will no longer be as necessary to read because the graphic layout will have an evident visual meaning. 'A picture is worth a thousand words.' The visual cortex, it is said, processes information much faster than does the part of the brain that reads words.

Nevertheless, the 'Thoreau Prototype' project, as its name affirms, is just that, an admirably conceived *prototype* for what will no doubt be an immense proliferation of such programmes and databases. This proliferation will transform humanities research in the coming years.

THE APORIAS OF CULTURAL STUDIES

Many of the features of the electronic book, made possible by the digitizing of audio, visual and alphabetic information, facilitate just the kind of research that is sought in cultural studies. Some of the same presuppositions are built into the cultural studies project. As in the case of Dada and film, so in this case the goals not of art but of scholarship have anticipated, and to some degree generated, the technological advances that will make it possible to reach them. But technological advance does not necessarily mean methodological sophistication or freedom from deep-seated ideological presuppositions. I see two interconnected ways of explaining the multi-media orientation of cultural studies and their concern for popular forms of art.

One is the transformation of ways of seeing, representing and accounting for social reality already effected by cinema, photography, the tape recorder and photocopy machines, as well as by the initial stages of the computer revolution. The direction in which software, digital storage methods, networking devices and search and retrieval mechanisms develop is encouraged in part by what scholars, among others, want to do with computers, not just by the intrinsic capabilities of the technology.

The other explanation for the appeal of cultural studies is the fact that the sensibilities of the, mostly younger, scholars who do such work have been formed by artworks and other cultural artefacts produced by the new technology. These scholars have been brought up on television, cinema and popular music on radio and on records, now on CDs and cassettes. They are the first generation for whom the book is not the primary source of cultural formation. Just as our students no longer read books but watch videos instead, so the scholars of cultural criticism are as adept in films, television, advertising, popular music and mass media generally as they are in the book. They are citizens of the new transnational culture that one encounters everywhere in the world today. The new technologies have made them, in part at least, what they are. No doubt all people, including scholars, have always mixed their responses to 'high' and 'popular' cultures, but the popular culture of today has features, for example its emphasis on visual signs, that may be having a particularly powerful effect on the way we interpret words of high culture of the past or present, especially literature.

I had occasion recently to hear both ends of a transcontinental telephone conversation between two university intellectuals in their late thirties. The conversation turned to popular music. These children of the Sixties, I discovered, have an extraordinarily detailed memory of the lyrics and various performances of a vast library of popular music. This music and the words that accompany it have had as much to do with making them what they are as all the books they have read, including all the works of theory in which they are so adept. Local linguistic, ethnic and regional societies still exist all over the world, but all of them are being irrevocably overlaid with (and changed by) the universal popular culture transmitted by radio, CDs, television and video, as well as by advertising in newspapers and magazines and by the myriad products of technological civilization: cars, aircraft, powdered milk, aspirin, and those ubiquitous blue jeans, tee-shirts and sneakers. This is as true for the traditional white Protestant culture of New England as for the traditional caste and multilingual societies of Nepal.

At this point the generous-minded scholar, cultural critic or not, rebels. Does the computer inevitably generate the ideology that accompanies its use? Is our scholarship fatefully determined by technology? Is there no way to appropriate the computer and its ancillary technology to change the university and move society toward a more just distribution of goods and power, just as Benjamin allows for the use of film for revolutionary ends? A way to answer these questions can be found by working through the aporias of the cultural studies project as such scholars as Abdul JanMohamed and David Lloyd define it. I shall do this in the light of the analogies I have identified between the themes of Benjamin's essay and the present situation of criticism and theory in relation to the digital revolution.

First aporia: Cultural studies presuppose the linguistic and ethnic specificity of any authentic culture, even though they would agree that all cultures to some degree overlap; otherwise we would not be able to understand alien cultures even as well as we do. The goal of cultural studies is not only to study marginalized cultures but to preserve and enhance them, to 'empower' them by institutionalizing their study in the university. Those who work in cultural studies want to use the university for archiving marginalized cultures and also for dismantling the hegemonic culture and replacing it with the now disempowered ones. Theory is used by cultural studies primarily as a means of deconstructing the dominant culture. The performative side of cultural studies lies in the way it not only describes but celebrates, preserves and enfranchises the now subordinate minority cultures for the sake of making possible their own self-determining change. Cultural studies presuppose that literature and other forms of art are embedded in the ethnic, linguistic and national identities from which they arise. They can only be understood in that context. That context, as I have said above, is both differentiated within itself and includes the damage done to the minority culture by the dominant culture. Though minority cultures can have validity and force outside that embeddedness, as they are appropriated by people in other subject-positions for other purposes, they are always in danger of becoming commodified if they are uprooted, in a process not unlike that loss of aura Benjamin describes. Cultural studies not only presuppose the explanatory power of such contextualizing, whether that contextualizing is linguistic, economic, gender-based, psychoanalytic or historical. Such studies also presuppose the preservative power of contextualizing. A work of art cut off from its ethnic and linguistic roots is in danger of withering and becoming like a dried flower in a collection or like an illustration in a botanical handbook. Cultural studies attempt to carry the soil along with the roots when the work is translated, transferred, moved to another place and another use, so keeping the work alive. On the other hand, such contextualizing may be in danger of smoothing over the specificity of a given work by relating it to an over-generalized model of its context. Examples might be the attempt to put Paul Klee back into Germany or Switzerland and explain him by showing how he is a specifically German or Swiss artist of a certain class and milieu, or the attempt to categorize Anthony Trollope as no more than a representative of Victorian, middle-class capitalist ideology aiding the police in their work of repression.[27]

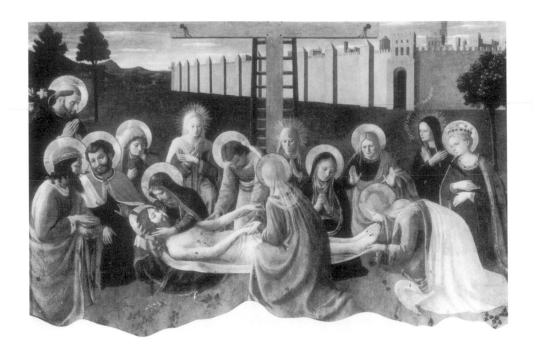

But this celebration of cultural specificity has occurred at a time when that specificity is being drastically altered by technological and other changes that are leading to internationalization of art and of culture generally. The work of cultural studies must be vigilant in order to avoid participating in that uprooting. The archival work that JanMohamed and Lloyd describes as one major facet of cultural studies is another form of the digital reproduction that may be in danger of putting everything on the same plane of instant availability, a symphony of Beethoven and African folk music, for example, or a Picasso or Fra Angelico and Chicano/a murals (illus. 10, 11). The illustrations to be found in this book are an example of that. They illustrate, and thereby do, what the book describes. By a paradox familiar to anthropologists, the effort of understanding, preservation and celebration may participate in the alteration of the cultures it would preserve. The more cultural studies try to save and empower local cultures for their own self-determining transformation, the more they may endanger them. Since the university is at present one of the most powerful institutional mechanisms for assimilating cultural diversity, how can cultural studies avoid participating in the work of assimilation

10 Fra Angelico, *Lamentation over the Dead Christ*, 1436.

46

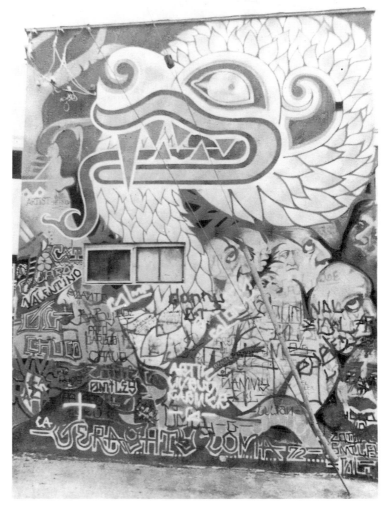

they would resist? Cultural studies recognize this danger in their emphasis on the need to transform the university, but, as they also recognize, the university has a great power of resistance to change and a great power of recuperation, as the reactionary backlash within certain élite universities today indicates.

Second aporia: Cultural studies have a double and contradictory orientation. As applied to subordinate cultures they are celebratory and preservative, archival, while at the same time seeking the productive transformation of those cultures. As applied to the dominant culture, they appropriate the procedures of critical theory to disempower that culture by showing its injustice and by showing the hidden ways in which a given work of art or literature was in spite of itself in the service of state power and state ideology. Stephen Greenblatt's work on Shakespeare and D. A. Miller's work on Victorian fiction are examples of this. The project of cultural studies depends in one way or another on the demand that social and intellectual justice be rendered to those who have been oppressed both by society generally and by the university. This demand is made in the name of the value of cultural difference. Even though cultural critics stress that these specificities must not be essentialized, important forms of cultural studies are carried on for the sake of the preservation of ethnic and gender identities.[28] Artworks and other cultural products are seen as growing out of those specificities. They are comprehensible only by being interpreted in relation to the context from which they have sprung. That is why it is so important to preserve and productively transform cultural differences.

Though this may appear disquietingly analogous in some ways to the concept of German art promulgated by the National Socialism of Nazi Germany and, in a significantly different way, by Martin Heidegger, the differences are as important as the analogies. The Nazis had absolute power within their own domain and wanted to impose on the whole world a single racial and national culture, whereas cultural critics speak in the name of those without power and would enhance cultural diversity. The Nazis essentialized race and national identities in a blindly mystified or perhaps sometimes cynically opportunist way, whereas many cultural critics have carefully thought through the distinction between ethnicity and nationalism, while stressing the need to resist essentializing concepts of ethnicity and emphasizing the diversity of nationalisms. As JanMohamed puts this:

> minority cultures (which are often but not always or necessarily 'ethnic' cultures) are, from our viewpoint, defined by their 'subject-positions', positions that are social constructs, and not by the essences of any 'race' or ethnic group as the Nazis would have it.[29]

Nothing could be further from the Nazi ideologues in political motivation, in subject-position, and in conceptual formulations than cultural critics like Lloyd and JanMohamed.

These are the days of a new conservative cultural nationalism. This is exemplified by the formation of the National Association of Scholars and by the explicitly politicized return in some universities to survey courses in 'the Western tradition', not to speak of the agendas of some who speak for the Government. The reinstatement of Western Civilization courses may go along with a restructuring of the humanities that diminishes 'peripheral' programmes like women's studies or African–American studies (a reduction often 'justified' by fiscal constraints). In such a situation the assault on the periphery by the centre in the name of a national aestheticism is without question a greater danger than the nationalist implications of some cultural studies on the margins. Nevertheless, until a practical alternative to nationalist ways of empowering disempowered minorities, that is, the invention of new kinds of group formations, is developed and shown to be workable, the danger of some form of nationalism will lurk as a dark possibility within the political project of cultural studies, just as essentialism or a return from analogical to digital thinking always remains as a possibility. As soon as you think of yourself as defined in important ways by your membership in some group, for example some disempowered minority, it is extremely difficult to avoid thinking of that group as having some essential rather than merely historical and contingent existence. And it is all too easy, even if you know nationalisms are contingent constructions, to justify some return to essentialist thinking on the grounds that political expediency justifies it. The challenge is to find ways to resist conservative nationalism without falling back on ways of thinking that generated the reactionary ideological aberrations in the first place. Only if the idea of the nationstate is itself put in question and transformed can this resistance hope to be successful. As cultural critics have recognized, many different kinds of nationalism and of nationalist solidarity exist. Not all of them presuppose territorial sovereignty, statehood and the assumption that citizenship is determined by birth, language and race, or some difficult process of assimilation, though certainly many forms of nationalism do presuppose that. But Benedict Anderson, for example, in *Imagined Communities: Reflections on the Origin and Spread of Nationalism* (1983) sees the sense of community as an imaginary fabrication constructed through literature and other cultural forms. The sense of community, to put this another way, always has an ideological component. The difficulty is to make that insight the basis of effective political action. Communities must be seen as contingent, always changing, the result of initiatory acts of allegiance. Those who ally themselves in this way must be willing to take responsibility for what they do in its name rather than appealing to some pre-existing group formation in whose name there is a right to act.

As Marx says in a striking aphorism: 'Whoever has a programme for the future is a reactionary.' How can Marx be shown by actual political and cultural action to be wrong in this? Practical and theoretical work in·this area is a major task for cultural criticism today. The aporia here is analogous to the use of terms like 'negation', 'dialectical' and 'sublation' to describe a non-binary opposition, whereas the terms carry within themselves binary implications. In the case of resistance to the dangers of nationalism, the aporia lies in the fact that all the vocabulary for naming and bringing about such new non-nationalistic kinds of group formations must be drawn from the nationalistic terminology that is being contested. The terms must be twisted to new uses and to new performative ends. That, as they say, takes some doing, as well as much vigilance, since nothing is easier than falling back into essentialist or nationalist thinking. The words we must use urge us to do that. My endpoint in this essay is to show how it may be possible to live within these dangers without succumbing to them, but the difficulty of doing so needs to be kept clearly in mind.

If one turns away from words to actual historical tasks, the problem does not go away. How, for example, can the culture of the Palestinians, the Kurds, the Croats, the Québecois of Canada or the Catholics of Northern Ireland be preserved and productively transformed as long as they do not have territorial and national sovereignty? Or, to give another example, in the city of Irvine, California, where I live, a total of fifty-nine different languages are spoken at home by its resident schoolchildren. What practical alternative is there to what is actually being done, that is, teaching them American English as quickly as possible, assimilating them into American, middle-class television-watching culture and thereby erasing the cultural legacies carried by those languages?

This second aporia lies in the fact that the more cultural studies work for the celebration, preservation, transformation and empowerment of subordinated cultures, the more they may aid in the replication of just those political orders they would contest. Certain conservative officials of the NEH or the Department of Education are right to be hostile to theory, since their business seems sometimes to be to keep us blindly within the ideology our cultural artefacts support, whereas cultural criticism is, or should be, a critique of ideology. It wants to wake us from the nightmare of history. But awaken us in the name of what? Or for the sake of what? To liberate us into that new digitized world of one universal culture that is, by traditional standards, no culture at all? Or to preserve, empower and transform unique local individual cultures? But that may have nationalistic consequences. Either of those directions seems a blind alley that must be avoided at all costs. Many cultural critics are fully aware of this problem and are attempting to think out ways in which cultural diversity may be preserved and enhanced without falling back into nationalistic strife.

This means inventing new forms of consolidation and solidarity, for example among women, or gays and lesbians, or Asian–Americans, forms that will work as means of giving power to such marginalized groups without falling back into some form of thinking in terms of self and other, us and them, or in terms of some pre-existing unity and right to power. Such thinking, paradoxically, makes it easier for the dominant culture in the university, in the mass media or in governmental agencies to appropriate cultural studies and the political movements for which they speak into some form of liberal pluralism, a pluralism that leaves the old power structures intact. A conception of group solidarity that sees each group as differentiated within itself and as constantly reinventing itself may be the way to resist this reappropriation. This would require the difficult effort, 'even during the heat of struggle . . . to abandon fixed ideas of settled identity and culturally authorized definition'.[30] It would also mean a radical challenge to conventional ideas of the state or nation, as well as of ideas of the community. Important work in this area has already been done, not only by Anderson but, for example, by Jean-François Lyotard, Jean-Luc Nancy, Maurice Blanchot and David Carroll.[31]

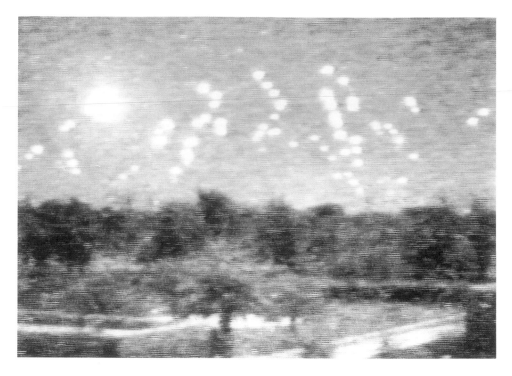

This second aporia may be approached from a somewhat different direction. As Benjamin astutely recognizes, 'all efforts to render politics aesthetic culminate in one thing: war. War and war only can set a goal for mass movements on the largest scale while respecting the traditional property system' (E, 241; G, 175). Benjamin's example is Marinetti's celebration of the beauty of the Ethiopian colonial war, but World War II was a spectacular confirmation of Benjamin's insight, as has been the television treatment of the Gulf War (illus. 12). Making aesthetics political, though it is essential to contesting the separation of the aesthetic realm from its material and social conditions by the dominant culture, may have a corresponding danger. One of the greatest menaces in Eastern Europe after the liberation of so many countries from Soviet domination is a resurgence of wars fought in the name of national or ethnic difference. Anti-Semitism is on the rise again in some parts of the former Soviet Union, or it has come out more openly now that various forms of policing are relaxed. In so far as the project of cultural studies is expressed in terms of hierarchies of power – hegemonic, white Euro-centric power as against the powerlessness of women,

12 *Desert Storm: The War Begins*, 1991, video-still of the bombing of Baghdad illuminated by tracer bullets.

minorities and Third World cultures – how can they avoid merely reversing the hierarchy, the putting out of power of those in power and the empowering of those now without power? Might this not replace one tyranny with another symmetrical one, or replace one inequitable distribution of property by another specular one? The means of this reversal might be some form of war. I mean a shooting war in which people are killed, property destroyed. Cultural studies must find some way to work for self-determination for all groups while not falling into the trap of this kind of nationalism. What would that way be? The conclusion of the first part of this book suggests answers to that question.

Third, and final, aporia: The project of cultural studies, as often formulated and practised, depends on the assumption that power and knowledge, the performative and cognitive aspects of such work, are symmetrical and harmonious. The knowledge of disempowered cultures gained by gathering, interpreting and storing literature, artworks and other products can go along with the practical political work of transforming the university and attaining power for the disempowered. But the performative and cognitive uses of language are never symmetrical. Just what will be the result of a performative use of language can never be cognitively foreseen, though one can be fairly sure that something will happen. To put this another way, the digital revolution may put us in a situation in which the distinction between cognitive and performative uses of language or other signs breaks down. Neither a pure performative nor a purely constative utterance ever existed in any case, but this fact may have a new pertinence when the work of archival storage becomes itself the performative transformation of the cultural expressions that may appear only to be in the process of being stored and known.

On one hand cultural criticism seeks to give knowledge of cultures, for example writing and art by women, or minority discourses. In so far as it gives knowledge, even knowledge generated by intimate sympathy and understanding, it might tend to neutralize those cultures by adding knowledge of them to the vast archives of the Western university as a basic institution of capitalistic and Eurocentric hegemony. That knowledge is theoretical through and through. Theory means knowledge. In so far as cultural criticism is performative, as its language indicates, in so far as it wants to change society and the university, to empower minorities or women, it is in danger of replacing one unjust and unjustified hegemony with another. Some people might say, 'So what? We have been oppressed for centuries and would like to do some oppressing ourselves. *Ecrasez l'infâme!*' But I doubt if many cultural critics would put it this way. They act to right centuries of injustice and to give a voice to the voiceless, the power of economic and artistic self-determination to the powerless. They act in the name of a universal justice.[32]

INAUGURATIVE RESPONSIBILITY

It will be seen that the three aporias of cultural criticism are versions of one another. Aporias can never be solved or escaped, only lived within and acted within in one way or another. The action does not erase the aporia. I shall conclude this part of this book by suggesting how cultural studies might act within these aporias in a way that would preserve and productively transform cultural difference in the new technological conditions while at the same time working for a more just social order everywhere. These are the basic goals of cultural studies. They have my wholehearted allegiance, but I agree with the cultural critics who recognize that these goals cannot be obtained by adopting the presuppositions about history, culture and the relations between culture and history of the hegemony that is being contested. Avoiding this involves vigilant and constant theoretical reflection – reflection, for example, about just what is involved in holding to that distinction between binary and analog(ue) opposition JanMohamed makes, or the effort to think through the difficult question of how to have differentiated cultural groups without falling back into one nationalism or another, or how to imagine self-determination without returning to Eurocentric ideas of individualism and subjectivity, or how to have power without injustice.

The elaboration of questions of responsibility and justice is a major task of cultural studies today. A contradiction inhabits the idea of performative praxis as it applies either to the cultural artefact or to the work of cultural criticism. On the one hand, performative praxis can be thought of as working on the ground of what already is – the pre-existing disadvantaged culture that is to be rescued and empowered. If it has such a ground, it is in danger of perpetuating the injustices of the past, even if only in the form of a symmetrical reversal. On the other hand, performative praxis can be thought of as inaugural, as bringing something hitherto unheard of into the world. For this the bringer must take responsibility. This responsibility cannot be grounded in anything that preceded the performative act of the artist or scholar, though it must at the same time be faithful to what it transforms. All effective performatives are of the latter kind, though they always mask themselves as the former. If so, much follows for the theory and practice of cultural criticism. Though the cultural critic always works from his or her own subject-position as a surrounding and limiting context, an inaugural performative, I claim, always exceeds its context, just as it is not amenable to being reduced to the deliberate act of a conscious, willing ego or 'I'. The I that says 'I claim', is created and made effective by the speech act it enunciates. All performatives are to some degree out of the control of the one who speaks them. The nature and effects of the performative dimension of cultural studies cannot be predicted, analysed, understood or determined by the pre-existing race, gender or class position of the one who speaks it.

My concept of artwork and scholarship as inaugural performatives is fundamentally different from what Heidegger says in 'The Origin of the Work of Art'. Heidegger opposes to the idea that art belongs to history or has a history the notion that 'Art is history in the essential sense that it grounds history [. . . *die Kunst ist Geschichte in dem wesentlichen Sinne, daß sie Geschichte . . . gründet*]'.[33] For Heidegger art is inaugural because it brings a pre-existing truth, the truth of Being, into the light. Art is also authentic for him only if it is the founding of a people:

> Whenever art happens – that is, whenever there is a beginning – a thrust enters history, history either begins or starts over again . . . History is the transporting of a people into its appointed task as entrance into that people's endowment. [*Geschichte ist die Entrückung eines Volkes in sein Aufgegebenes als Einrückung in sein Mitgegebenes*] (E, 77; G, 64; the translation loses the play on words ending in '-*rückung*' and '-*gegebenes*' here).

The disasters of national aestheticism and aesthetic national-ism are latent in such formulations, in spite of the fact that Heidegger, unlike the Nazis, does not see art as the deliberate tool of the makers of the aesthetic state but as a founding revelation of Being that 'happens'.

I mean something quite different from what Heidegger means when I argue that we should see the artwork and the work of cultural criticism as inaugural. Rather than being the revelation of pre-existing Being, what both art and criticism reveal is themselves. This is a particular, idiomatic configur-ation of meaning that cannot be fully accounted for by the personality and intentions of its maker, nor by the surround-ing culture, nor by the antecedents in the tradition to which the work belongs. Nor is it univocal. It is divided within itself by the presence of its own other. It differs from itself or within itself. The cultural context must be studied not in order to melt the work back into it, but as an indispensable analysis undertaken to identify the differentiae that make the work different and different from itself. This difference means that the work, whether of art, popular culture or criticism, changes the society into which it enters, makes it, in however minute a way, begin again. The work in its difference is trans-formed again when it is subjected to the work of cultural criticism that is attempting to generate newly empowered forms of group solidarity.

As Drucilla Cornell has argued apropos of the relation of judicial decision to law and justice, such a view of the way cultural events are performative presupposes a sense of time and therefore of history different from the usual linear time of a series of presents – the once present, the present present and the future present. Time, rather, is riven by difference in the present. It is the locus of the constant invention and intervention of something wholly other. Time is, therefore, the perpetual remaking of the past in the name of the future that not only is not yet but that has never been, a future of radical novelty.[34] Actions performed within such a time are inherently violent. They are a violence without ground, like all truly inaugural gestures, as Benjamin argues in 'The Critique of Violence'.[35] The risks of such violence are obvious, but these risks must be taken if the pre-programmed continuation of the injustices that already exist is to be avoided.

For the results of such violent actions both artist and cultural critic must say 'Yes, I did it', even though the effect of what they do can never be certainly foreseen. The work of the cultural critic, like the cultural products she or he studies, can and should be performed in the name of a justice and democratic equity that have not yet come into the world and that can now only be indistinctly imagined. Such appeals cannot escape the impasse of seeming to depend on standards or concepts that pre-exist the appeal, here 'justice' and 'democratic equity', standards that are part of the contested hegemonic culture. But the work of cultural criticism can transform and then reinscribe these terms in a founding gesture that is without precedent or ground. Such constitution of a ground cannot justify itself by appeal to a pre-existing right to cultural autonomy or to political power. The work of artist or of cultural critic is a response to an infinite demand not only from a heritage to which the artist or critic must be faithful, but from the 'other' of that heritage. That heritage is already inhabited by its other. Its other is within, not outside. All cultures were and are constantly changing, always differing from themselves. They do not exist as a single, monolithic unity. This is as true of the dominant culture as of marginalized ones. The demonstration that this is the case with the canonized Western tradition remains one of the major tasks of cultural studies, along with the empowering of marginalized cultures. Only such a demonstration can dismantle the mystified ideological assumption that there is a unified 'Western tradition' forming a solid ground for our institutions.

Both artist and critic respond to a demand that we take responsibility for the cultural past, in all its diversity, in the name of a more equable future that our work helps bring into existence. This relation to the past may be defined as 'remembering the future'.[36] In its work for social and institutional change, cultural criticism can learn much from the brilliant performative rewriting within legal studies of so-called Deconstruction, or, it might be better to say, Deconstructions, since Deconstruction is by no means a univocal form of discourse.[37] An example is the distinction Drucilla Cornell makes between law mechanically applied, therefore always unjust, and true justice, in which the judge always remakes the law, even though she or he must obey it.

From the perspective of this view of the cultural critic's responsibility, the computer and its associated technologies appear potentially democratic. The computer does not dictate the uses we make of it, however much it may provide the matrices for our work. We still have to choose the materials we want to use from the vast repertory available. We still have to select the paths and procedures that assemble the materials we have chosen, and we still must read the materials, in the strong sense of the word *read*. This reading includes both the artefact, its context and the links between them. Even in the case of visual or auditory signs, the word *read*, in its emphasis on an interventionist and productive activity of interpretation that takes nothing for granted, is still the best word available. To abandon the great advances that have been made in the reading of verbal texts, not to work on the problem of how these procedures can be translated to the reading of visual and auditory materials, on the grounds that the goal is now different, or that the materials are not all made of words, or that reading is a sterile, self-enclosed narcissistic activity, would be a serious mistake. Without some grounding in procedures of verification, for which rhetorical reading offers the best precedents, the cultural critic might be free to say anything she or he likes about the film, the piece of advertising, or whatever. Not only can no fixed frontiers be drawn between artefact and context,[38] but the relation between the two, as well as the 'link' between, is always some form of a sign to sign relation, not a relation of sign to thing, nor a matter of direct physical causality. The sign to sign relation, moreover, is always a matter of distance and difference. The work operates a transformation of its material, historical, social or ideological context that is fundamentally figurative. It might be called a perpetually iterated anamorphosis of the real. This transformation is not transparent. It always demands to be read.

But who is this 'we' who does the reading? What is the gender of this 'we'? How does sexual difference enter into its constitution? And what force can be given to the words 'select' and 'choose' I have used here? It is a we beyond the old notions of the pre-existing ethically obligated subject. It is even beyond the idea that the 'I' is socially constructed once and for all along with its gender, subject position, class and race. The we is the collective subject of an infinite and impossible responsibility. This subject is brought into existence by the performative political act that incurs the responsibility. This would include gender, class and race. If these are socially constituted, they are constantly being reconstituted by the acts of the self-constituting we. The age of digital reproduction imposes a new kind of freedom, the freedom that goes with the instant availability within electronic space of a vast archive. This freedom goes also with the inherent neutrality, for example, of Boolean search techniques, even though all these technologies can be programmed to produce foregone and even oppressive conclusions. The inapplicability of old concepts of the scholar as private I to work done on the computer, co-operates with other more overtly political changes to replace the individual I with a new kind of we. But 'we' do not yet have adequate conceptual and legal ways of understanding this new kind of we and protecting its rights, since our laws and concepts, such as those of authorship and copyright, were developed around the idea of the autonomous individual subject. Important work is already being done in the area of copyright, for example by Peter Jaszi and Martha Woodmansee. Work on the general question of new concepts of gender and of the subject is already active in cultural studies, for example in women's studies or in investigations of the colonial subject.

'Our' freedom comes back again in the end to the responsibility to read, to read all sorts of signs and to criticize them or make them effective again in the present. This responsibility is both political and ethical. It can justify itself by no appeal to precedent, no established procedures of reading, nor can it blame the text or work for what we do with it, even though what happens in reading happens. As the just judge must reinvent the laws, even though she or he must be faithful to them, so the cultural critic must posit anew, as something new, the culture that is studied, while at the same time being faithful to it. This positing also recreates the critic. To some degree it transforms his or her subject-position, for example by implicitly or explicitly changing the scholar–teacher's relation to the institution that pays him or her. Such a double contradictory demand is both logically impossible to fulfil and absolutely necessary to fulfil. Responding to it is the first obligation in cultural criticism.[39]

In part Two of this book I shall illustrate this with a discussion of illustrated novels, or, more generally, works juxta-posing picture and word. Questions raised in the discussion of cultural studies in the first part of this book return obliquely throughout the second part, for example questions about pro-cedures necessary to read multi-media works, about the subject-position of the critic and her or his responsibility for the effects of what she or he writes, about the need to resist essentializing and hierarchizing tendencies, and about the performative dimension of the act of reading cultural artefacts in any medium or mixture of mediums. For the most part I shall let my readings of pictures and words speak for them-selves, but some connections between the first and second parts of this book will be explicitly indicated. Most of all I attempt to show the particular difficulties involved in 'read-ing' any work that juxtaposes words and visual images. This includes, of course, a great many of the works studied by cultural critics: films, television, advertising, illustrated maga-zines and books, photographs with captions or with words within the photographic image.

Part Two: Word and Image

Je suis pour – aucune illustration . . . (Mallarmé)[40]

The sun . . . is new each day. (Heraclitus)[41]

IMAGES ET TEXTE

Illustration – the word means bringing to light, as a spelunker lights up a cave, or as a medieval manuscript is illuminated. What is the function of illustrations in novels? Many novels, especially in the nineteenth century, were, in their original appearance at least, provided with illustrations. A new branch of the interpretation of fiction has recently been opened up by the recovery, for example, of the graphic tradition to which Dickens's illustrators belonged and by the study of Dickens's novels as multi-media collaborative productions.[42] This attention to illustrations in novels has no doubt in part been stimulated by discussion of the relation of picture and word in film studies.[43] The new interest in the illustrations for nineteenth-century novels is a good example of Walter Benjamin's thesis, in 'The Work of Art in the Age of Mechanical Reproduction', that new technological means of reproduction have transformed the way we see artworks of the past. Ours is a visual and a multi-media age, the age of cinema and television. This, it may be, has led to a new recognition that nineteenth-century novels also combined two kinds of signs. More broadly, the theoretical issue that lies behind the function of illustrations in novels is the relation of picture to word. Is a picture worth a thousand words? If so, why? Perhaps because the picture presents something, makes it more present, than any words can, and does this more economically. A picture leaves language following lamely behind with its fatal necessity of enumerating things one by one. Perhaps.

Mark Twain did not think a picture superior to text. In a splendidly exuberant passage in *Life on the Mississippi* Twain argues for the helplessness of picture without word. A picture presents something, but what that something is cannot be known for sure unless the picture is labelled, placed back within the context of some diachronic narrative. The interpretation of a picture is, for Twain, necessarily verbal. Without some explicit indication in words of what frozen narrative moment the picture represents, the spectator vibrates back and forth among contradictory alternative stories. The picture might be illustrating any one of them:

In this building [the Washington Artillery Building in New Orleans] we saw many interesting relics of the war. Also a fine oil painting representing Stonewall Jackson's last interview with General Lee. Both men are on horseback. Jackson has just ridden up and is accosting Lee. The picture is very valuable, on account of the portraits, which are authentic. But, like many another historical picture, it means nothing without its label. And one label will fit it as well as another:

First Interview Between Lee and Jackson.
Last Interview Between Lee and Jackson.
Jackson Introducing Himself to Lee.
Jackson Accepting Lee's Invitation to Dinner.
Jackson Declining Lee's Invitation to Dinner – With Thanks.
Jackson Apologizing for a Heavy Defeat.
Jackson Reporting a Great Victory.
Jackson Asking Lee for a Match.

It tells one story, and a sufficient one; for it says quite plainly and satisfactorily, 'Here are Lee and Jackson together.' The artist would have made it tell that this was Lee and Jackson's last interview, if he could have done it. But he couldn't, for there wasn't any way to do it. A good legible label is usually worth, for information, a ton of significant attitude and expression in a historical picture. In Rome, people with fine sympathetic natures stand up and weep in front of the celebrated 'Beatrice Cenci the Day Before her Execution'. It shows what a label can do. If they did not know the picture, they would inspect it unmoved, and say, 'Young Girl with Hay Fever'; 'Young Girl with her Head in a Bag'.[44]

In the polemic, or *paragone*,[45] between show and tell, Twain comes down firmly on the side of tell. A picture is 'authentic' if it is copied from life. It may then be a genuine representation of a historical event. But there is no way to tell exactly

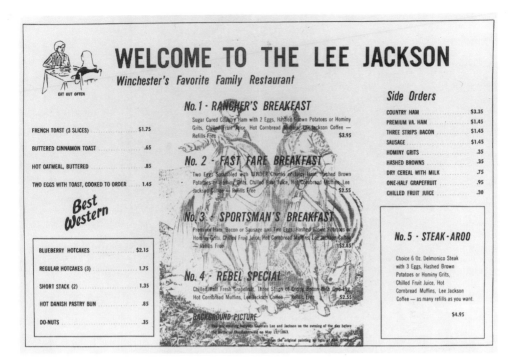

13 Breakfast place-mat, from the Lee Jackson Motel, Winchester, Virginia.

what that historical event was and how it fits into a narration unless the picture is firmly 'labelled'. This is just what Benjamin was to argue in the essay on 'The Work of Art' discussed above. The rest of this book is an investigation by way of examples of his claim and Twain's. In order to be comprehensible, both say, a picture must plainly illustrate a story. Words are necessary to indicate what story it is.[46]

When I read the passage in *Life on the Mississippi* I was anxious to see the picture for myself, to see whether the painting is really as indeterminate as Twain says. Several years ago I was staying in the Lee Jackson Motel in Winchester, Virginia. There on the breakfast place-mats, with the menu printed over it, was a reproduction of my painting (illus. 13). Attempts to find the painting itself and to see it or a reproduction were unsuccessful. Later I visited the Lee Chapel at Washington and Lee University in Lexington, Virginia, the location of Lee's mausoleum. In the shop at the Chapel was a large collection of reproductions of the painting: there were postcards and various tinted engravings, as well as large posters of it. Research at the University library located the painting and its provenance (illus. 14). I learned

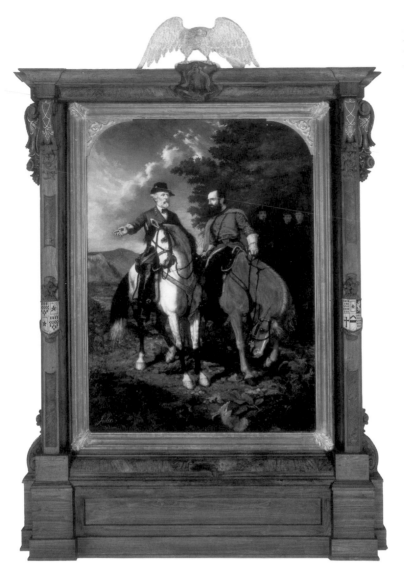

14 Everett B.D. Julio, *The Last Meeting of Lee and Jackson*, 1869.

that engravings of the painting were hanging in many Sou-
thern homes after the Civil War. The painting no doubt
seemed a poignant embodiment of a lost cause that might
have been won had Jackson not been killed.[47] The last interview between General Robert E. Lee, the leader of the Confederate Army, and General 'Stonewall' Jackson, his chief
subordinate, took place near Winchester, on the morning of
the Battle of Chancellorsville, 2 May 1863. It was the last
meeting because Jackson was mortally wounded by accident

by a Confederate sniper later that day, after the Confederàtes had won the battle. The name of the motel no doubt commemorates this meeting. I shall say no more of these pieces of serendipity, except to agree with Twain that it is impossible to tell from the picture alone exactly what moment in what story it illustrates, or who the people are, though the choices and prices on the breakfast menu are clear enough. By telling a little story of my own about it I have given it another label and incorporated it within another narrative.

The admirable Edward Gorey, master of horrid inconsequentiality, exploits, like Twain, the resources for black humour of the indeterminacy of pictures, but in a somewhat different way. His sequences of drawings with captions tell stories all right, though exceedingly strange ones, for example, *The Unstrung Harp; or Mr Earbrass Writes a Novel, The Doubtful Gas, The Insect God*, or *The Hapless Child*. Other sequences are organized according to the absurd order of the alphabet, for example *The Fatal Lozenge* or *The Gashly Crumb Tinies*. Most relevant for my purposes are sequences that present pictures with captions placing them within a narrative of which the other parts are missing. Examples are *The Object Lesson* and *The Willowdale Handcar; or the Return of The Black Doll* (illus. 15). There seems to be a story going on behind the scenes in the firmly labelled pictures in each sequence, but that story is constantly interrupted by false clues. *The Willowdale Handcar* provides an example. The picture is well described by its caption: 'During the thunderstorm that ensued, a flash of lightning revealed a figure creeping up the embankment.'[48] The creeping figure is never identified in any later pictures or captions, nor is he (it seems to be a he) connected in any identifiable way with what comes before or after. The sequence seems to tell some obscure story of the seduction of Nellie, though that story may be created by lines of connection the reader draws retrospectively, without justification, between disconnected moments. The flash of lightning brings something to light in the white, forked fissure left blank in the midst of the black cross-hatching, but exactly what that something is there is no way to tell. The caption describes but does not explain.

The effect of such a picture with explanatory caption is strange. It shows that even verbal narratives are made of synchronic segments that are obscure when their causal links

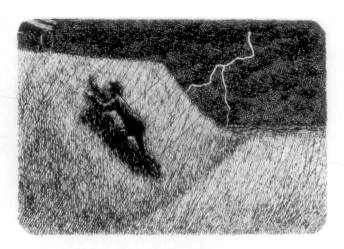

*During the thunderstorm that ensued, a flash
of lightning revealed a figure creeping up
the embankment.*

to before and after are broken. The power of a picture is to
detach a moment from its temporal sequence and make it
hang there in a perpetual non-present representational present, without past or future. The power of presentation in
an illustration is so strong that it suspends all memory and
anticipation inscribed in words, for example in the necessary
allusion to temporality of verb tenses in captions. If Gorey's
pictures in *The Willowdale Handcar* are in an eternal present,
the captions are in the past. A picture, labelled or not, is a
permanent parabasis, an eternal moment suspending, for the
moment at least, any attempt to tell a story through time.

If graphic illustration has such disruptive power, has – as
Svetlana Alpers has argued[49] – the interpretation of pictures
been illicitly invaded by models of reading based too narrowly
on the kind of meaning written words have? Is there a mode
of meaning specific to the graphic image, exceeding,
supplementing or lying beside any meaning that can be
expressed in words, therefore irreducible to any words, however eloquent? This would presumably be, as Alpers argues,
some mode of presentation that the graphic arts accomplish
and that is in no way possible through words. The latter are
by nature the presence of an absence. In the presence of the
thing itself words are not needed. A painting is there, here
and now. It brings something into light, before our eyes.

Robert Browning has Fra Lippo Lippi argue just this. Fra Lippo echoes the traditional priority, going back to Plato and Aristotle, of the visible, the theatrical, the mimetic, the spectacular in the process of learning:

> God's works – paint any one, and count it crime
> To let a truth slip. Don't object, 'His works
> Are here already; nature is complete:
> Suppose you reproduce her – (which you can't)
> There's no advantage! you must beat her, then.'
> For don't you mark? we're made so that we love
> First when we see them painted, things we have passed
> Perhaps a hundred times nor cared to see;
> And so they are better, painted – better to us,
> Which is the same thing. Art was given for that . . .[50]

Stéphane Mallarmé recognized this power in pictures, but he feared it rather than, like Browning, praising it. 'I am for – no illustration', says Mallarmé, 'everything a book evokes having to pass into the mind or spirit of the reader' (*tout ce qu'évoque un livre devant se passer dans l'esprit du lecteur*).[51] The words on the page have a performative power of evocation. They make present in the spirit something otherwise absent. If that power is distracted, drawn off in a detour, diverted into an illustration (presumably after passing first into the mind of the illustrator), it will then not operate where it ought, on the spirit of the reader. It will pass into the picture and be present there. The text will be impotent to work its magic effect of evocation on the mind of the reader, calling forth spirits within it. A book, it seems, has only so much magic energy. An illustration will drain this power off, leaving the book dead letter, short-circuited by the superior power of the illustration to make something present. The book has always been no more than dead letter, since its power is the power of evocation, a raising of the dead. The word evokes. The illustration presents. *makes present what has past*

Mallarmé, with however much or little irony, follows his rejection of graphic illustration for books with the remark that if you substitute photography for the traditional illustration in etching or engraving, why not go all the way to cinematography. Here his little essay, like Twain's remarks, prefigures Benjamin. Cinema, in its unrolling along a temporal axis of narration, will to advantage replace both the texts and illustrations of many a volume: 'que n'allez vous droit au cinématographie, dont le déroulement remplacera, images et texte, maint volume avantageusement' (ibid.). This comment is a prophecy, accurate enough, of the power cinema has enjoyed in displacing the illustrated book. What Mallarmé says is also an ironic recognition that there are many books which in no way exploit the particular evocative power of the printed word and therefore might as well be replaced by the 'movies'. The key word in Mallarmé's formulation is *replace*. Photographs were, in Mallarmé's time, replacing the older graphic arts as the medium for book illustration. Photographs were, in turn, replaced by cinematography, one form of graphing or graving rapidly substituting for another, leaving the power of the written word farther and farther behind. Finally, words are present only as the subsidiary remnant of subtitles in silent movies. Even these were no longer necessary when the talkies were developed, in the final triumph, so it seems, of the visual and auditory over the written word. Just as John Ruskin's hatred of the photograph (expressed in *Ariadne Florentina*, for example) was in the name of the superior representative power of engraving, so Mallarmé's ironic tribute to the obliterating power of illustration over text is in the name of something only the written word can do, something all his own work attempts to exploit in its naked purity.

Henry James, in his correspondence with Alvin Langdon Coburn about the photographic frontispieces for the 'New York' edition of his novels and in the discussion of these photographs in the preface to *The Golden Bowl*, took a different view. He saw photographs as acceptable illustrations because they were 'in as different a "medium" as possible'.[52] Nevertheless, James shares Mallarmé's fear that illustrations will usurp or darken the illuminating power of the text. The words on the page, in James's view as in Mallarmé's, have as their prime gift the ability to evoke images, to conjure them into being: 'The essence of any representational work is of course to bristle with immediate images'; it 'put[s] forward illustrative claims (that is, produce[s] an effective illustration) by its own intrinsic virtue' (p. ix). The reader is reduced, sometimes, to 'such a state of hallucination by the images one has evoked' that he cannot rest until he has made a 'semblance of them in his own other medium'. But those illustrations of what is already, if it has any value, sufficiently illustrative on its own, are entirely alien to the text and should stand off from it, keep out of its light.

The images James uses for the danger that graphic poses to verbal are obliquely illustrative themselves. They are taken, oddly enough, from gardening and eating. Gardening is like illustration in that in both cases something comes into the light out of an obscure ground. The elucidation of the graphic would interfere with the free growth of the verbal illustration, shade it, stunt it. So it must be kept at a distance:

> his [the author's] own garden, however, remains one thing, and the garden he has prompted the cultivation of at other hands becomes quite another; which means that the frame of one's own work no more provides place for such a plot than we expect flesh and fish to be served on the same platter (p. x).

A novel with pictures is like a garden growing two incompatible crops. It is a frame enclosing not only its own shapely design but also an alien parasitical plot, plot as garden and plot as artistic design or story. Or it is a plate offering two inharmonious foods, or, in a final variation, it is a plant on which is grafted a foreign stock:

> I, for one, should have looked much askance at the proposal, on the part of my associates in the whole business, to graft or 'grow', at whatever point, a picture by another hand on my own picture – this being always, to my sense, a lawless incident (p. ix).

'Graft' and 'graphic' of course have the same Greek root, *graphein*, to write. In the case of grafting this is from the pencil-like shape of the sharpened shoot inserted under the bark of the parent stock. A grafted tree producing both yellow and red apples is 'lawless', a monster or *lusus naturae*.

Why, if he so fears the alien power of illustration, does James show such 'inconsistency of attitude in the matter of the "grafted" image' as to share with Coburn in the delightful search for appropriate scenes to photograph for the frontispieces for the 'New York' edition? The photographs must simultaneously, and somewhat inconsistently, be as separate from the text as possible, echoing it at a distance, while at the same time slavishly dependent on it, and also, still at the same time, asserting their own power of bringing to light something not in the text but out there in the real world. James's idea was that the photographs were 'not to keep or to pretend to keep, anything like dramatic step with their suggested matter' (p. x). They would be rather 'images always confessing themselves mere optical symbols or echos, expressions of no particular thing in the text, but only the type or idea of this thing or that thing' (p. xi). They were to be 'pictures of our "set" staged with the actors left out' (p. xi).[53] An example of this procedure is Coburn's photograph of a curiosity shop as an illustration for *The Golden Bowl* (illus. 16). The photograph shows neither people nor that sun-like half-sphere, with its hidden crack, that is James's prime symbol of the secretly flawed relations among his characters.

16 Alvin Langdon Coburn, *Curiosity Shop*, photograph, from *The Golden Bowl*, 1909.

As James's gingerly comments indicate, he knew he was playing with fire, the fire of a possible excess of visual image over text, a 'competition' of the one with the other. In *A Small Boy and Others* he observes that for him when he was a child Dickens's *Oliver Twist* meant more the powerful etchings by Cruikshank than Dickens's text. The illustrations, for him, obliterated the words. James tries to avoid this danger by thinking of the photographs as in no way pictures of specific passages in the text. Moreover, the people are to be entirely left out, as in the photographs by Atget of empty Paris streets that Benjamin discusses. Photographs can present settings, background, such as the curiosity shop, but not minds, feelings, persons in their interaction. The latter is the business of words. The photographs are 'optical symbols' not of the text but of 'types' or 'ideas'. The latter stand above both image and text as something each points toward in its own special way. Image and text echo one another at a safe distance. Their resonance is guaranteed by their equal relation to a third thing both bring to light in different ways. Each photograph illustrates, makes visible, not this or that detail in the text, but a general type or idea that the text magically evokes, as Mallarmé says. Each photograph would thereby be kept subsidiary to the text, in no danger of overwhelming it. The photograph imitates the text at a double remove. It represents not its signs nor its referent, but its significance, its impalpable *signifié*.

Another passage in the preface to *The Golden Bowl* expresses James's wavering, his double theory of photographic illustrations. On the one hand he holds that the photographs echo

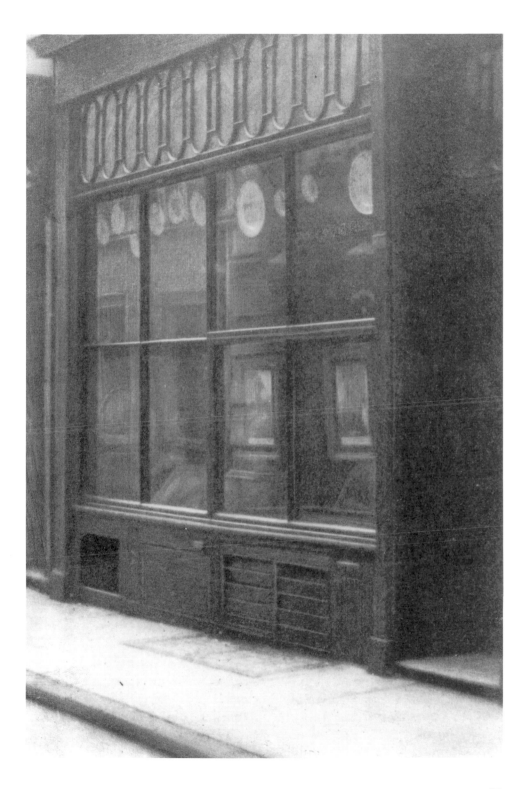

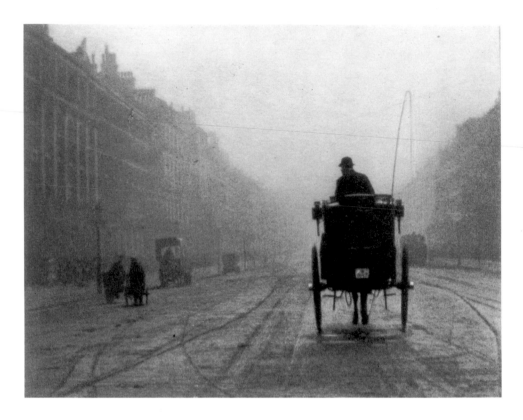

at a distance something in the novel. On the other hand, he holds that they speak for something in the objects they picture, thereby making present within the covers of the book something alien to the text. His idea, he says, held up as a 'light' to the city of London for Coburn's illumination, was

17 Alvin Langdon Coburn, *Portland Place*, photograph, from *The Golden Bowl*, 1909.

> of the aspect of things or combinations of objects that might, by a latent virtue in it, speak of its connection with something in the book, and yet at the same time speak enough for its odd or interesting self (p. xi).

An example of this is *Portland Place* (illus. 17), the other photograph for *The Golden Bowl*. The 'latent virtue' is not in the photograph, but in what the photograph represents, in the visible aspect of real things. This virtue brings into the open not only something exposed in another way by the words of the book but also something separate, something proper to itself. All James's work, it could be shown, turns on the undecidable question (which nevertheless urgently needs deciding) of whether the type or idea pre-exists its representation in picture or word, or is present in something the representation copies, or is generated by the representation. Much is at stake in his not wholly consistent attempt to adjudicate the relation between picture and dramatic word in the 'New York' edition of his novels. A similar question arises in the attempt within cultural studies today to decide whether the words and images of popular culture and the mass media are constitutive of our culture or only mediate pre-existing ideological formations.

Images et texte – Mallarmé's phrase identifies the place of a warfare between the two media, in the full spectrum of its possible skirmishes, from the true blue of pure text at one end to the reddest red of pure representational image at the other, if such purity exists. At one end text seems wholly dominant, the literary text entirely without pictures other than those it intrinsically 'evokes'. But some poems are also, strangely, pictures, like George Herbert's 'The Altar' or Mallarmé's 'Un coup de dés', or William Carlos Williams's 'The Yellow Smokestack', or 'pattern poems' by John Hollander in *Types of Shape*, for example 'Swan and Shadow'. Such texts are calligrams. The words are arranged to make a representation of what they talk about. Michel Foucault has, in *Ceci n'est pas une pipe*, admirably articulated the way René Magritte's paintings deconstruct the calligram and turn mimetic 'resemblance' into serial 'similitude' beyond the hierarchy of real original and secondary copy.[54] Concrete poetry of our own day also belongs to this tradition. Calligrams seem intended to show that the words on a page can do anything pictures can. After all, both text and image are something seen with the eyes and made sense of as a sign. What, in fact, is the difference between reading a word and making sense of a picture? This is just the question.

The spectrum continues with literary works that discuss graphic works not given as such, like Henry James's *The Sacred Fount, The Ambassadors,* or so many other works by him, or like the episode of Sam Weller's Valentine in Dickens's *The Pickwick Papers.* Toward the middle of the sequence from verbal to graphic are illustrated novels, works where the two media are presented side by side, but with text still dominant. This balance shades off, in the other direction, to graphic works, perhaps in narrative series, that have printed words as titles, subtitles or commentary, for example *The Pickwick*

Papers as it was originally conceived, namely as a series of etchings accompanied by Dickens's subsidiary 'letterpress', or, to give another example already mentioned, the stories in pictures by Edward Gorey. In these cases picture and word have relatively equal force, as they do in the work of William Blake or D. G. Rossetti.

Moving now toward the other extreme, some pictures have accompanying verses. Examples are paintings by J. M. W. Turner that he illustrated by passages he claimed were from his own long poem, 'The Fallacies of Hope', though the poem exists only as fragments. Word is also subordinate in paintings that have a title as ironic or incongruous accompanying label, for example the witty and enigmatic titles that Paul Klee appended to his paintings. These titles are in Klee's own hand and thereby become an inextricable part of the painting itself, like Klee's signature. Like the signature, the titles are both graphic and verbal at once, since they have a decorative or calligraphic value. They are a painting of the words. The same thing in another way can be said of those late paintings by Klee that represent rows of what seem to be either primitive drawings or letters in some unknown and as yet undeciphered alphabet (illus. 18). In these figures picture and word

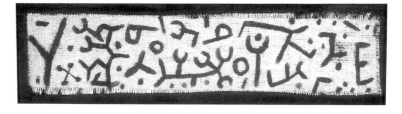

18 Paul Klee, *Ohne Titel (Schrift)*, 1940.

seem to come together at the origin of both. These strange signs are not yet either pictures or letters. They are the originating point where both coincided before their separation into the different sign functions of picturing and writing. Another form of the subordination of writing to picturing are paintings that represent the act of writing, like those Dutch paintings Svetlana Alpers has discussed,[55] or paintings that have words or letters in one way or another as part of the picture, like so many twentieth-century paintings from Cubism on. At this extreme, finally, are pictures that are, so it seems, nothing but picture. These have, apparently, nothing whatsoever of writing about them. They are purely graphic, in one sense, and therefore entirely without graphic elements, in the other sense. It may be doubted, however, whether such purity can exist.

What is the ground of this *polemos* within the graphic? The warfare in question is present within the word 'graphic', which can refer either to writing or to picture. Could peace be established between the two parties by showing that they are different forms of the same thing, as blue and red are both light? What would that 'something' be?

RUSKIN

A way toward an answer to these questions may be found by asking another, apparently much easier, one. Why did John Ruskin call his lectures on the art of engraving *Ariadne Florentina*?[56] What does Ariadne have to do with engraving? Trying to answer these questions will lead us through a maze of images and citations all making the distinction between picture and word problematic. Ruskin makes the distinction problematic by relating both words and pictures to the primordial material act of scratching a surface to make it a sign. That sign, Ruskin suggests, is always a miniature maze and is always connected to its context by labyrinthine lines of filiation. Moreover, each assembly of signs, for Ruskin, expresses in one way or another love, war and death, or is bordered by these as things no sign can signify other than indirectly. For Ruskin, not only are signs always both verbal and pictorial, but also any configuration of signs has a temporal and narrative dimension. To trace out a sign is to tell a story.

Ruskin defines engraving as 'the Art of Scratch' (p. 320). 'To engrave', he says, 'is, in final strictness, "to decorate a surface with furrows." . . . A ploughed field is the purest type of such art: and is, on hilly land, an exquisite piece of decoration' (p. 322). To find the explanation of the title *Ariadne Florentina*, readers must make their way to the end of the last lecture. The answer leads back through the lectures to other works by Ruskin, and beyond them, to all their pretexts, in labyrinthine intricacy:

The entire body of ornamental design connected with writing, in the Middle Ages, seems as if it were the sensible symbol, to the eye and brain, of the methods of error and recovery, the minglings of crooked with straight, and perverse with progressive, which constitute the great problem of human morals and fate; and when I chose the title for the collected series of these lectures, I hope to have justified it by careful analysis of the methods of labyrinthine ornament, which, made sacred by the Thesian traditions and beginning in imitation of physical truth, with the spiral waves of the waters of Babylon as the Assyrian carved them, entangled in their returns the eyes of men, on Greek vase and Christian manuscript – till they closed in the arabesques which sprang round the last luxury of Venice and Rome (pp. 450–1).

The sentence is a splendid labyrinth in itself, but it gives the reader the clue to follow. Writing as arbitrary sign grows, for Ruskin, out of pictures, for example those schematic Assyrian representations of waves as mazes. In the paragraph that follows the one just quoted, Ruskin describes an old, embroidered silken sampler of scenes from the life of Abraham on the wall of the hotel room in Lancaster where he is revising his lectures. 'Such work as this', says Ruskin, 'means the patience and simplicity of all feminine life' (p. 453). Needlework, patient and intricate, woman's work in Ruskin's sexist view, is like the labyrinthine intricacy of engraving or of biblical or Greek storytelling. Engraving may therefore be put, along with weaving and embroidery, under the double aegis of Penelope and Ariadne:

> the spirits of Penelope and Ariadne reign vivid in all the work [of the sampler] – and the richness of pleasurable fancy is as great still, in these silken labors, as in the marble arches and golden roof of the Cathedral of Monreal (p. 453).

Weaving, needlework, ornamental arabesques on illuminated manuscripts and medieval architecture, modern engraving – all come together in being labyrinthine in form and in representing the intricacies of the moral life. The Cretan labyrinth, with its associated story of Ariadne, Theseus and the Minotaur, always represents moral choice for Ruskin, for example in the references to Ariadne in *Fors Clavigera*.[57] The retracing of the labyrinth by Ariadne's thread is a kind of writing, as is Penelope's weaving.[58]

Ruskin recognizes that labyrinthine ornamental design has always been 'connected with writing', as in illuminated capitals or in *The Book of Kells*. He understands that there is an element of picture in every letter, and an element of writing in every picture. In an illuminated capital the one flows into the other. They are superimposed or interwoven. The place where one stops and the other begins can scarcely be detected. Where would one put an illuminated capital on my spectrum from pure picture to pure letter? It seems to be at both ends at once, therefore the locus of a battle between the extremes.

Ruskin's reference to 'Thesian traditions' is a remembering of that 'crane dance' in which the Cretan labyrinth was marked out on the ground by the maze-like movements of the dancers. This dance is a form of engraving, the cutting of a furrow making a design on the earth. In association with the crane dance Ruskin recalls the medieval English game of equestrian winding and turning. The latter echoes the *Ludus Trojae* in Virgil's *Aeneid* (v, 588), and still remains as a maze marked out at Troy Farm in Oxfordshire. Ruskin recalls also the 'quaint mazes in the wanton green', worn into the earth by the 'tread' of the 'nine-men's morris' in *A Midsummer Night's Dream* (II, i, 98),[59] and the 'labyrinth of Ariadne, as cut on the Downs by shepherds from time immemorial' (p. 134). All these are examples of dancing or mock war as a way of engraving on the earth a sign that is also a design.

A splendid passage in the *Aeneid*, v, describes the funeral games for Anchises. The passage shows that these mock wars and puberty rituals continued from century to century and from culture to culture in response to some deep need. They are the marking out of a living and moving labyrinth modelled on some presupposed Cretan labyrinth of stone:

They say that once upon a time the labyrinth in mountainous Crete contained a path, twining between walls which barred the view [*in alta / parietibus textum caecis iter*], with a treacherous uncertainty in its thousand ways, so that its baffling plan, which none might master and none retrace, would foil the trail of any guiding clues [*qua signa sequendi / falleret indeprensus et inremeabilis error*]. By just such a course the sons of the Trojans knotted their paths, weaving in play their fleeing and their fighting [*textuntque fugas et proelia ludo*], like dolphins that swim through the sea-water.[60]

Love and war; love as war; play; game; dance as mock war; war turned to war-game and therefore to dance; the to and fro, give and take, approach and withdrawal of sexual combat in courtship – these are figures for the temporal movement of some life story. Retrospective narration is then the re-tracing of a spatial design already there. That spatial design has been left as remnant after the events are over. The meaning of such remnants is created magically, after the fact, when the results of an action that marked the world are seen. All narrative, Ruskin's figure suggests, tells the story of the mazy turnings and returnings, 'the methods of error and recovery, the minglings of crooked with straight, and perverse with progressive', of the moral life. The labyrinth of narrative is generated by the interference of error and truth, ignorance and knowledge, that makes up each story of love or war. Sexual differentiation is presumed in all stories. That differentiation generates the long human story of love and conflict. Every particular narrative, even something as far from the *Aeneid* as Dickens's *The Pickwick Papers*, is an example of this development of narrative from difference. In the traditional gendering of acts that are like the sex act, the act of fissuring a surface with a stick, engraving a furrow, the art of scratch, is seen as male; the act of weaving some fabric as a cover for nakedness is seen as female.[61] Both writing and engraving come together, for Ruskin, beyond such conventional gender distinctions, in this double act of engraving and embroider-ing, uncovering and covering, unveiling and veiling, pen-etrating and hiding, illustrating and darkening, engraving in the double sense of burying a corpse and scratching out a design; weaving is double too: Penelope's weaving of her web both defers her choice among the suitors and makes a shroud for Ulysses's father, Laërtes.

The *Ludus Trojae* were funeral games performed by young boys of Sicily and Troy for Aeneas's dead father, Anchises. The maze traced out by the horsemen was elegiac. It was a throwing away of what was already gone and a re-establish-ment after death, the death of the father, of the productive rhythms of life. Does not Freud connect writing, which for his culture then was the pouring out of a liquid from a cylindrical instrument, with the treading out of a measure on the maternal earth, and with the sex act, particularly a forbidden, incestuous sex act? The latter is seen, as is usual with Freud, from the male perspective. If incest is taboo, its surrogates may by displacement become impossible too, so that walking or writing may also be blocked.[62]

Freud's dark equations may seem a long way from Ruskin's theory of engraving as the art of scratch, and a long way too from the question of why Ruskin gives his book such an odd mythological title. But no reader of Ruskin can doubt that for him all the threads of human concern are woven into one fabric. Any line, for example that primordial 'first' line scratched on wood, stone or earth by the first engraver, will, if followed where it leads, reach out, in labyrinthine windings, to the whole design of human existence – art, technology, morality, politics, warfare, economics, epistemology, metaphysics.[63] For Ruskin, writing or making a picture are material acts, acts inseparable from the most fundamental events of life. His emphases are consonant with the assumptions of those cultural critics who see the making or using of any cultural artefact as an active and constitutive part of the life of that culture, materially embedded in it, never just a representation of it.

HEIDEGGER

The reader will, perhaps, already have noticed the resemblance between Ruskin's theory of engraving and Martin Heidegger's thought, in 'The Origin of the Work of Art', about the *Riß* (trait or fissure), the *Zug* (drawing or abstraction), the *Zeug* (production) and the *Gezüge* (the system that holds the traits together in a design), with all their related families of words.[64] Like Ruskin, Heidegger associates the fissure, or *Riß*, made by the engraver's tool with the furrow made by a plough in the earth. For Heidegger too, such a fissure makes a design that is a bringing to light, an illustration. Heidegger adopts the Greek word *aletheia* for this. *Aletheia* is revelation, bringing the truth into the open. Such illumination is, for Heidegger, the basic function of the work of art, whether the work is graphic, architectural, verbal or the product of craftsmanship (as in the making of a pot or a pair of shoes).

Jacques Derrida has in 'Restitutions'[65] discussed at length what is problematic in Heidegger's remarks in 'The Origin of the Work of Art' about Van Gogh's painting of the pair of shoes (illus. 19). For Derrida, it is not even certain that the shoes are a pair, and far from being the shoes of a peasant woman of the Black Forest, they are probably Van Gogh's own shoes, as Meyer Schapiro was the first to assert. Heidegger made two self-revealing mistakes, a mistake about gender and a mistake about class. Nevertheless, if one wants to read the most distinguished modern expression of the idea that something otherwise hidden is revealed in a special way in the graphic arts, made present there, the somewhat labyrinthine track of Heidegger's essay is the path to follow. We can witness the power of Van Gogh's painting, says Heidegger, 'only by bringing ourselves before Van Gogh's painting'.[66] When we placed ourselves before the painting, 'This painting spoke [*Dieses hat gesprochen*]. In the vicinity of the work we were suddenly somewhere else than we usually tend to be' (G, 24; E, 35). Heidegger says nothing about whether a reproduction would also 'speak' in this way. Presumably not. As for Benjamin, so for Heidegger: only the original will have aura, or 'speak'. For both, this power is associated with distance. Van Gogh's painting takes us 'somewhere else [*jäh anderswo*]'. Though Heidegger elsewhere in the essay ascribes to the language of poetry a similar power of bringing the truth into the open, the 'speaking' of Van

Gogh's painting is peculiar to the power of visible paint on the canvas. It is not something that depends on language or on speaking as such, though it is a form of speaking. It is mute speech, not something that can be duplicated in words. The painting is not a mere illustration of something else that could just as well be seen and understood without it. Only this painting speaks what this painting speaks. What it speaks is truth, but it is not the truth of this particular pair of shoes that is copied or represented by Van Gogh in the painting. It is the truth of what a product, a man-made useful object, in itself is, its essence or being. The German word translated somewhat awkwardly into English as 'equipment' is one of the family of 'Zug' words: *Zeug*, product, something drawn into existence by human work. 'The work, therefore', says Heidegger, 'is not the reproduction of some particular entity that happens to be present at any given time; it is, on the contrary, the reproduction of the thing's general essence' (E, 37; G, 26). If the painting is not mimesis in the sense of copy, it is not illustration or demonstration either:

> . . . above all, the work did not, as it might seem at first, serve merely for a better visualizing of what a piece of equipment is. Rather, the equipmentality of equipment [*das Zeugsein des Zeuges*] first genuinely arrives at its appearance [*Vorschein*] through the work and only in the work (E, 36; G, 25).

This appearance, or *Vorschein*, Heidegger goes on to say, in formulations that are at the centre of his theory of the artwork, is the bringing into the open of the truth of equipmentality (*Zeugsein*), or, to phrase it better, the Being of the work:

> What happens here? What is at work in the work? Van Gogh's painting is the disclosure of what the equipment, the pair of peasant's shoes, *is* in truth [*in Wahrheit ist*. This phrase can mean both 'in fact is' and 'is in relation to the Truth of Being']. This entity emerges into the uncon-cealedness of its being. The Greeks called the uncon-cealedness of beings 'aletheia' (E, 36; G, 25).

Abstracted in this way from the intricate argument of 'The Origin of the Work of Art', Heidegger's doctrine of what is at work in the work appears to be an exceedingly elegant formulation of the 'aesthetic' view of art, with its roots not only in Greek thought, but, closer to hand, in the aesthetics of Kant and Hegel, with their differing emphases on *Schein*, *Erscheinung*, *Vorschein*, all that family of words indicating shining, coming into the light, as the essence of the work of art. An example is Hegel's celebrated formula in the *Aesthetik*, cited above, about the Beautiful as 'the sensible appearance [*Scheinen*] of the Idea'.

Another modern parallel to Heidegger's idea about the shining forth of the work of art would be Benjamin's concept of the 'aura' in his essay 'On Some Motifs in Baudelaire' and in 'The Work of Art in the Age of Mechanical Reproduction'. Benjamin's 'aura' has already been discussed above and has formed the basis of my investigation here. Like Kant, Hegel or Benjamin in their different ways, Heidegger believes that the work of art testifies to its authenticity by its shining, as though it were a little sun in itself. 'Some particular entity', says Heidegger, 'a pair of peasant's shoes, comes in the work to stand in the light of its being. The being of the being comes into the steadiness of its shining [*in das Ständige seines Scheinens*]' (E, 36; G, 25).

As Derrida has recognized, Heidegger wavers back and forth between various ways of reading Van Gogh's painting. It is by way of one of these waverings that we can find a track back to the topic of engraving and ultimately back to Ruskin. The wavering wobbles around a double axis. One involves the relation of the painting to the shoes. Sometimes, as in the passages I have been quoting, Heidegger seems to be saying that something is at work in the work itself that makes the shining. Sometimes he seems to be saying, like Browning, that the painting is necessary to bring into the light a shining that the shoes have in themselves, before they are painted, though that shining is obscured by the everyday use of the shoes. Something is at work in the work of making the shoes that is analogous to what is at work in the painting of them, though this is obscured and needs the painting to bring it out, so to speak. 'But perhaps it is only in the picture', says Heidegger, 'that we notice all this about the shoes' (E, 34; G, 23). Sometimes Heidegger speaks as though the shoes do not need the painting at all but shine sufficiently in themselves, particularly if they are put back into the context of the 'world'

(*Welt*), to use Heidegger's term, of work and living in which they belong.

The shoes are one means of creating the world of the peasant woman to whom they belong. The shoes stand forth as an item in that world. This creation involves the heavy work of ploughing, sowing and reaping, the diurnal and annual course of the sun, the treading out of the path or furrow in the heavy earth that is ultimately the track from birth to death. The passage describing the peasant shoes in their context is one of Heidegger's grandly orchestrated evocations of peasant life. Perhaps in its pathos it verges on the sentimental or the condescending, or on that danger always present when an intellectual glorifies the life of obscure toil, for example Claude Lévi-Strauss in *Tristes Tropiques*, or Joseph Conrad in *The Nigger of the Narcissus*. It is even a danger in some current work in ethnic studies and 'minority discourse'. Moreover, if Meyer Schapiro is right, Van Gogh actually painted his own shoes, not those of a peasant woman. If so, the full pathos of the peasant woman's life is projected into the painting by Heidegger himself. Finally, if one thinks of what was happening in the Germany of that time, the triumph of National Socialism and the vast industrial mobilization and preparation for World War II, the notion that German society was still one traditional Black Forest life of immemorial peasant toil and production has a sinister and disquieting resonance. Here is the passage:

> From the dark opening of the worn insides of the shoes the toilsome tread of the worker stares forth. In the stiffly rugged heaviness of the shoes there is the accumulated tenacity of her slow trudge through the far-spreading and ever-uniform furrows of the field swept by a raw wind. On the leather lie the dampness and richness of the soil. Under the soles glides the loneliness of the field-path as evening falls. In the shoes vibrates the silent call of the earth, its quiet gift of the ripening grain and its unexplained self-refusal in the fallow desolation of the wintry field. This equipment [*Zeug*] is pervaded by the uncomplaining anxiety as to the certainty of bread, the wordless joy of having once more withstood want, the trembling before the impending childbed and shivering at the surrounding menace of death. This equipment belongs to the earth and

is to be protected in the world of the peasant woman. From out of this protected belonging the equipment itself rises to its resting-within-itself [*Aus diesem behüteten Zugehören ersteht das Zeug selbst zu seinem Insichruhen*] (E, 33–4; G, 22–3).

As for Ruskin, so for Heidegger, though with a markedly different tonality, the primal furrow marked out on earth by some form of utensil brings into the open and holds together there the whole human world of birth, work, love-making and death, the rising and setting of the sun, the turning of the seasons. For Heidegger, as other essays make clear, the human world is the product of a fourfold tension among earth, sky, man and the gods.[67]

I said that what Heidegger proposes wavers around a double axis. But each axis wavers in itself. The first axis is the question of the relation of the painting to what it represents. On that topic Heidegger says now one thing, now another. The second wobbling pivot is the profound ambiguity, in all Heidegger says, about whether the marking out of the furrow creates something or only reveals it. Heidegger usually seems to be unequivocally affirming the latter, but the haunting possibility of the former inhabits all his work like the ghost of another light, invisible in the daylight of the apparent shining of Being. Something comes to light in a work, something is at work in the work, whether in the making of a work of art, or in the making of a product, a pair of shoes, or in the ploughing, sowing and reaping of the peasant, or even, it might be added, in the tracing out of Heidegger's philosophical arguments in the book to which 'The Origin of the Work of Art' belongs, *Holzwege*, 'forest paths'. This title is rendered in the French translation as *Chemins qui ne mènent nulle part* (Paths that Lead Nowhere). A *Holzweg* is a woodcutter's path that goes into the forest and stops, peters out. It is not a way to get from here to some definite 'there'. So in this essay, what cannot be told for certain is whether the work makes the light or whether it unveils a light already there but hidden. Everything, nevertheless, depends on which is the case, including the political authority that might be justified if the light really is already there, but might be unjust tyranny if the illumination is only imposed arbitrarily from the outside. As Philippe Lacoue-Labarthe and others have demonstrated, the political state is for Heidegger and for the whole tradition of 'German aesthetic ideology' another work analogous to the work of art or to the work of philosophy.[68] Heidegger, in a passage in 'The Origin of the Work of Art' already cited in part above, says unequivocally that art is not only within history but grounds, or inaugurates, history:

> As founding, art is essentially historical. This means not only that art has a history, in the purely exterior sense that in the course of time it, too, appears side by side with many other phenomena and is subject to processes of transformation whereby it emerges and disappears, offering thus to the science of history a series of changing aspects. Art is History in the essential sense that it grounds History (E, 77; G, 64).

This assertion, however, can have two profoundly different meanings. It may mean that art grounds history in the sense of bringing into the light a new revelation of Being. In that case the culture or political state inaugurated and supported by the new work of art would have the authenticity of something with a firm foundation outside itself. On the other hand, Heidegger's formulation may mean that the work of art is without its own grounds outside itself but nevertheless inaugurates history, culture and the state by a groundless performative fiat, by invention not revelation. In that case the state so founded would be without transcendent grounds and so could be seen as inauthentic, shallow and tyrannical, unless the founders, as I have argued above, are willing to take full responsibility for the new state they inaugurate.[69] The resistance to Fascism depends on assuming that the latter is the case, but only at the risk of possibly depriving art of any but a superficial role as ideological superstructure in a democratic state.[70]

As Jean-Joseph Goux has shown, this question focused, for Heidegger, on the status of modern art.[71] In one of his last lectures, 'The Origin of Art and the Determination of Thinking', given in Athens in 1967, Heidegger asked 'from what region comes the exigency to which modern art, in all its domains, responds?' The answer is that modern art is no longer rooted in the language of a particular people or nation. It responds to the global civilization being produced by technology. The works of modern art, no longer emerge marked by the seal of the limits of a world defined by the people or the nation. They belong to the universality of global civilization. Their composition and their organization are part of that which scientific technology projects and produces.[72]

It would seem to follow that global technology has replaced the language of a people or a nation, essential means of the revelation of Being, as the ground of art. But here Heidegger hesitates, in an extraordinary, prolonged moment of indecision, since to allow art to become global would undermine all his claim that art is the inaugural ground of a genuine national culture. This indecision, I am arguing, was already obliquely present in 'The Origin of the Work of Art', and forms a fundamental oscillation in Heidegger's thought. Here is indeed a path that leads nowhere:

> . . . one is easily prompted to explain that the region from which the requirement to which modern art responds is none other than the scientific world.
>
> We hesitate to give our assent. We remain in indecision.[73]

For Heidegger too, as for Ruskin, understanding engraving as a way of making a picture can take place only in the context of these questionings of the ground and social function of art. The primal engraving is the ever-uniform furrows of a ploughed field. Engraving as such, an engraving by Dürer, for example, is only a version of ploughing, scratching or marking. It is subject to the same laws and comprehensible only in the same context. In a passage providing a concentrated example of Heidegger's play on the family of words drawn from *Riß*, Heidegger brings in Dürer's 'Art of Scratch' (to remember Ruskin's phrase) as an example:

> Someone who is bound to know what he was talking about, Albrecht Dürer, did after all make the well-known remark: 'For in truth, art lies hidden within nature [*steckt die Kunst in der Natur*]; he who can wrest it from her, has it.' 'Wrest' means to draw out the rift and to draw the design with the drawing-pen on the drawing-board (E, 70; G, 58).

Heidegger's word-play is lost in translation here, not only the give and take among the *Riß* family of words but also the vibration between *Riß* as fissure already there and *Riß* as design made by the artist. In order to preserve the word-play on *Riß*, Heidegger emphasizes Dürer's work in drawing rather than his engravings and woodcuts. The words translated as 'rift' and as 'design' in the English translation are in German the same word (*Riß*) with two meanings coming and going within it: 'Reißen heißt hier Herausholen des Risses und den Riß reißen mit der Reißfeder auf dem Reißbrett.'

The rift sets boundaries and gives measures, as well as fissuring and dividing. The rest of the paragraph exposes further the unstillable oscillation between thinking of the *Riß* as latent originally in nature and only brought into the open by the work of art, and, on the other hand, thinking of it as something that is originated in the work and has no prior existence. 'True', says Heidegger, 'there lies hidden in nature a rift-design, a measure and a boundary [*steckt in der Natur ein Riß, Maß, und Grenze*] and tied to it, a capacity for bringing forth – that is, art.' Art is here, as for Aristotle or for Wallace Stevens, both part of nature, that part of nature which has to do with mimesis as revelation, and at the same time something that supplements nature, since without art the *Riß* would remain concealed. 'But it is equally certain', continues Heidegger, 'that this art hidden in nature becomes manifest only through the work because it lies [*steckt*] originally in the work' (E, 70; G, 58). The play from one possibility to the other is in the word *stecken*. The *Riß* is both the cleft of an abyss opening into 'nothing' (in Heidegger's sense of that word: nothingness as a manifestation of Being), and at the same time the sharp incised line, the 'trait' making a design that is a meaningful sign, whether letter or picture.[74] The design which is also a crack, canyon or ravine is both always already 'stuck' in nature, therefore only exposed by the artwork and at the same time is 'stuck' originally ('ursprünglich') in the work by the work. If the latter, the design is created by the work and laid as a pattern over nature, as something superficial, alien to it, like the pattern of furrows ploughed in parallel curving lines on a hill. On the one hand, the work of art adds something to nature. On the other hand, the working of the work is part of nature. Art is in nature, 'Kunst [ist] in der Natur', and at the same time art originates something, is in itself an 'Ursprung', rather than springing from one.

What it might mean to say that art is 'stuck' in nature, Ruskin's comments on *The Last Furrow*, a woodcut in the series *The Dance of Death* by Holbein, as well as the woodcut itself, will make more manifest, that is, illustrate. (Holbein's designs for *The Dance of Death* and others were, in fact, cut in Basle by Hans Lützelburger. Ruskin apparently did not know this: he speaks of the work as all Holbein's.) 'This vignette' (illus. 20), says Ruskin:

> represents a sunset in the open mountainous fields of southern Germany. And Holbein is so entirely careless about the light and shade, which a Dutchman would first have thought of, as resulting from the sunset, that, as he works, he forgets altogether where his light comes from. Here, actually, the shadow of the figure is cast from the side, right across the picture, while the sun is in front. And there is not the slightest attempt to indicate gradations of light in the sky, darkness in the forest, or any other positive elements of chiaroscuro . . . It is Holbein's object here to express the diffused and intense light of a golden summer sunset, so far as is consistent with grander purposes (pp. 352–3).

Ruskin's remarks here are part of a polemic against the attempt to represent chiaroscuro in any engraving, in wood or on steel, but, beyond that, what does *The Last Furrow*, for Ruskin, bring to light? As is usual with him, there is in his mind a complex argument involving the technical aspects of making a certain kind of artwork, the morality of art, its economy and its relation to ultimate truth. In this case death, gold and the sun, in a systematic interrelation, are the carriers of these ideas – that sun whose daily disappearance into the earth is a kind of death, gold the colour of sun but also the measure of truth and value, as the sun is the source of bodily and mental energy. 'Quite seriously', says Ruskin in *The Eagle's Nest*,

> all the vital functions, – and, like the rest and with the rest, the pure and wholesome faculties of the brain, – rise and

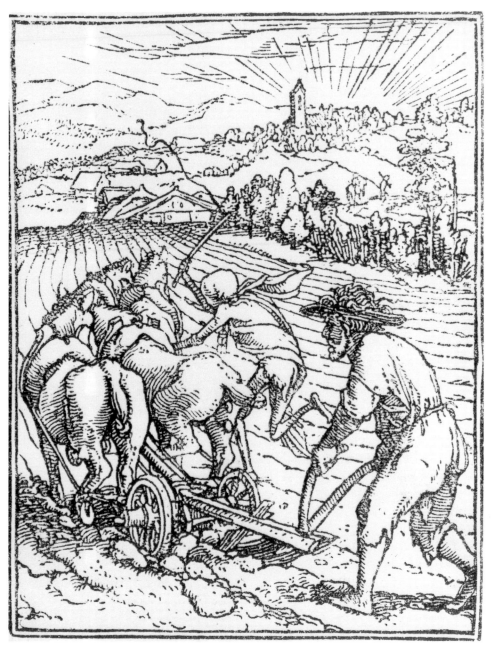

20 After Hans Holbein the Younger, *The Last Furrow*, woodcut, from Ruskin's *Ariadne Florentina*, 1906.

set with the sun: your digestion and intellect are alike dependent on its beams: your thoughts, like your blood, flow from the force of it, in all scientific accuracy and necessity. 'Sol illuminatio nostra est; Sol salus nostra; Sol sapientia nostra.'[75]

The attempt to represent chiaroscuro in woodcut (as also in engraving, though for slightly different reasons in each case), is a false use of the technical capabilities of the medium, since picturing by woodcut is best if strong and firm lines are used: 'the virtue of wood engraving is to exhibit the qualities and power of *thick* lines' (p. 350). The attempt to represent chiaroscuro in wood is uneconomical. It is a waste of the valuable time of the cutter or engraver in the vain attempt to falsify the natural penchant of the medium. The attempt to do so produces false gold, or gold mixed with lead, 'base coin, – alloyed gold' (p. 357), as in Tenniel, whereas Holbein's work is 'beaten gold, seven times tried in the fire' (ibid.). Where Holbein – Ruskin thought it was Holbein – lays one line, Tenniel has a dozen. This means that Holbein is never in a hurry and always does each line as best he can, whereas Tenniel is always in a hurry, 'everywhere doing things which he knows to be wrong' (p. 358). Holbein's work, in short, is not only economical, but moral, whereas Tenniel's is uneconomical, in every sense, and immoral.

Ruskin's animus against chiaroscuro, for example as it is used in Rembrandt's etchings, is something like Goethe's animus against Newton's optics or like Turner's motives for appropriating Goethe's theory of colour, to be discussed below. Much is at stake here. The interpretation must proceed carefully among these analogies, feeling its way slowly along the line of the proffered clue. According to Ruskin, the trouble with the attempt to represent light and shade in woodcut is that it is necessarily based on a shade that is totally black. This domination of black is not only unpleasant but false, false physically and metaphysically, whereas true light draws its source from the sun and shades off toward less light or diffused light, as in Holbein's sunset scene. The attempt to present chiaroscuro in woodcut

> implies the idea of a system of light and shade in which the shadow is totally black. Now, no light and shade can be good [this word must be taken both in a moral and in

21 Thomas
Bewick, *Frog*,
wood-engraving,
from Ruskin's
Ariadne Florentina,
1906.

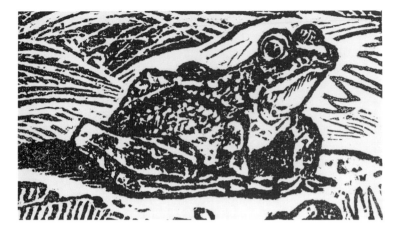

an aesthetic sense], much less pleasant, in which all the shade is stark black. Therefore, the finest woodcutting ignores light and shade, and expresses only form, and *dark local colour* (p. 351).

What is dark in a good woodcut is not black, but the representation of one or another form of light, that is, some dark colour, as in the splendid frog by Bewick that Ruskin reproduces and discusses (illus. 21), in which, as he says, 'you know at once that . . . the frog [is] brown or green' (p. 365).

The starkness and firmness of outline in Holbein's *The Last Furrow*, 'blunt lines; . . . quiet lines, entirely steady' (p. 356), in which all is strongly either black or white, is to be associated with Holbein's Protestant and Reformist temper. Holbein not only sees all things in the light of truth, but distinguishes sharply good and bad, right and wrong. 'The teaching of Holbein', says Ruskin,

> is therefore always melancholy, – for the most part purely rational; and entirely furious in its indignation against all who, either by actual injustice in this life, or by what he holds to be false promise of another, destroy the good, or the energy, of the few days which man has to live . . . he is never himself unjust; never caricatures or equivocates; gives the facts as he knows them, with explanatory symbols few and clear (p. 354).

Holbein's 'Dance of Death is the most energetic and telling of all the forms given, in this epoch, to the *rationalist spirit* of reform, preaching the new Gospel of Death, – ''It is no matter whether you are priest or layman, what you believe, or what you do: here is the end"' (p. 353).

In the case of *The Last Furrow*, says Ruskin, 'the meaning is . . . plain'. But Ruskin does not quite bring out into the open, in his commentary, what that meaning is:

> The husbandman is old and gaunt, and has passed his days, not in speaking, but in pressing the iron into the ground. And the payment for his life work is, that he is clothed in rags, and his feet are bare on the clods; and he has no hat – but the brim of a hat only, and his long, unkempt grey hair comes through. But all the air is full of warmth and of peace; and, beyond his village church, there is, at last, light indeed. His horses lag in the furrow, and his own limbs totter and fail: but one comes to help him. 'It is a long field', says Death; 'but we'll get to the end of it to-day, – you and I' (p. 355).

'I have, God woot, a large feeld to ere / And wayke been the oxen in my plough', says the Knight in *The Canterbury Tales* ('The Knight's Tale', 886–7). This passage in Chaucer connects ploughing with writing or storytelling, just as Ruskin connects it with engraving both as the carving of a design and as burying. If Ruskin is right to say that all the air in this woodcut is full of a 'diffused warmth' (p. 353) whose representation is made possible precisely because Holbein does not try to show light and shade, ·nevertheless this warmth is about to disappear. The sun is setting, even though it is setting behind the village church, the promise of another light in another world. The farmer is ploughing his last furrow, both in the sense that it is the last of the day, as the light fails, and in the sense that he is walking with Death down the last furrow toward his own imminent demise. If the parallel lines of the furrows on a hill make an elegant design, an example of what Ruskin calls the purest type of engraving, the line made by the farmer, his plough, the four horses and the whip-handle flourished by Death curves round from lower right to mid-left to upper right, across the grain of those ploughed furrows, and leads straight toward the disappearing sun. The ploughing of the furrow seems to be making a fosse in which to bury the sun. The line begins outside the two border lines on the lower right, where that invisible other black sun, the double of the one that has just set, sheds its shadow on man, horse and plough. The whole curve goes from invisible sun to invisible sun through a middle line where the light, its source and what it illuminates, man and his whole environing world of work and art, are there, out in the open, like the journey of a day or a life.

In another doubling, the furrows cut by the farmer's plough are represented by the furrows in the wood cut in reverse by the knife. Or the furrows represent the cuts by the knife, in an oscillation back and forth from what is pictured to the art of making a picture. That this doubling of the represented scene by the process of representation is not a fanciful association on my part, but was already part of Ruskin's theory of engraving, is demonstrated by a passage in the beginning of Ruskin's chapter on 'The Technics of Wood Engraving':

> The instrument with which the substance, whether of the wood or steel, is cut away, is the same. It is a solid plough-share, which, instead of throwing the earth aside, throws it up and out, producing at first a single ravine, or furrow, in the wood or metal . . . The furrow produced is at first the wedge-shaped or cuneiform ravine . . . (p. 348).

The word 'cuneiform', meaning wedge-shaped, here reminds the reader that one of the original forms of writing, Babylonian cuneiform, was made by cutting marks with a wedge-like instrument in clay tablets that were then baked in the sun. This writing is a form of ploughing.

Writing, the engraving of pictures in wood or steel, the ploughing of a field – all three are versions of the same act of making incisive marks on matter that creates signs and their significances. This act is a double simultaneous movement of bringing to light and burying, carving a grave, by engraving, for the sun and making a pattern. All writing, engraving and ploughing go from darkness to darkness, from death to death, and what they bring into the open at the same time they hide. They bury the sun. They also bring the sun, or at any rate the double of the sun, a represented sun, into the open. One of the horses in *The Last Furrow* manures the field it helps plough. The making of the furrow that curves toward the vanishing-point where the sun has set is for the sake of planting the seed that will bring new life once more out of death as the months pass and the sun rises and sets daily. 'That which thou sowest is not quickened, except it die' (I Corinthians 15:36).

This double movement of revealing and hiding, of appearing and disappearing, in the production of a work of art, in writing and in work, is governed, for Holbein, for Ruskin, and later for Heidegger, by the double movement of the sun. 'The luster and gleam of the stone [*Der Glanz und das Leuchten des Gesteins*]', says Heidegger (in 'The Origin of the Work of Art') of a temple,

> though itself apparently glowing [*anscheinend*] only by the grace of the sun, yet first brings to light [*zum Vor-schein*] the light of the day, the breadth of the sky, the darkness of the night . . . The Greeks early called this emerging and rising in itself and in all things *phusis*. It clears and illuminates [*Sie lichtet*], also, that on which and in which man bases his dwelling. We call this ground the *earth* . . . Earth is that whence the arising brings back and shelters everything that arises without violation (E, 42; G, 31).

Heidegger's thought here presupposes that concept of the tension and interplay among four elements, man, earth, sky and gods, worked out in most detail in 'The Thing'.[76] For Ruskin, as for Heidegger, illumination or illustration results from an interaction among the basic elements of our world. Though the diffused, warm golden light in Holbein's woodcut seems to come from the sun, in fact it belongs to the wood, itself born of the earth, which the plough-shaped chisel or gauger of the woodcutter has helped cut. The light is produced by that act of cutting. It arises magically from the play of black and white lines and spaces when the pattern on the block is stamped in reverse on paper, and then, by a long series of relays, reproduced in facsimile in Ruskin's book or in the slide that can be cast on a screen in a lecture hall.

Of the reproduction of Holbein's *The Last Furrow* for *Ariadne Florentina* by 'Mr Burgess', Ruskin says: 'The toil and skill necessary to produce a facsimile of this degree of precision will only be recognized by the reader who has had considerable experience of actual work' (p. 352). Throughout this long series of productions and reproductions, black on white and white on black, from Holbein to Lützelburger to Burgess, Holbein's sun still shines indirectly from below its horizon. It is brought out over and over by the interaction of lines and spaces between the lines in the illustration, whatever its size or medium, just as the meaning of a word is generated by the black marks on a white page, for example in this sentence, and is transmissible from copy to copy of the text, handwritten, typed or printed in fonts of different design and size.

Holbein's woodcut is dialogical. In spite of Holbein's rationalist Reformist faith, his work is subject to a double sun and a double logos, the logos of the sun as earthly manifestation of God, pictured in the picture, and the logos of that other sun the artwork actually generates. The interference of picture and text with one another, *their* dialogical relation, in any situation in which they are set side by side, arises not from the fact that they are different media that produce meaning differently, but from the fact that they work in the same way to produce meaning, as designs that are signs. A picture and a text juxtaposed will always have different meanings or logoi. They will conflict irreconcilably with one another, since they are different signs, just as would two different sentences side by side, or two different pictures. Only the same can mean the same. Neither the meaning of a picture nor the meaning of a sentence is by any means translatable. The picture means itself. The sentence means itself. The two can never meet, not even at some vanishing-point where the sun has set.

If each expression or stamping out in each medium means itself, that meaning, as all my examples – graphic, verbal, critical and philosophical – demonstrate, is never univocal. Each meaning is itself subject, like Holbein's *The Last Furrow* or like Heidegger's doctrine in 'The Origin of the Work of Art', to a double sun, a double logos. This twofold hypothesized source of meaning makes each separate expression, picture or text, dialogical within itself, therefore double in meaning.[77] The warfare between media is doubled by an internal warfare intrinsic to each medium in itself.

This double doubling may be variously defined. The doubleness may be located in a heterogeneity between media that is doubled by a duplicity within each sign or conglomeration of signs in any medium. It may be located as a failure of any sign to be self-identical or univocal. The doubleness may be defined as an irreducible residue of non-meaning or of materiality in any sign or collection of signs in any medium. Any sign is to some degree meaningless or possessed of a unique non-repeatable or untranslatable meaning. In this each sign is like a proper name. Or, to propose a final formulation, it is not only the case that any visual image is other than, the 'other' of, its accompanying words. Each expression in each medium is also inhabited by its own other. The difficult, perhaps impossible, task of reading works in either medium consists, in part, of identifying in each case this other by way of tracks it has left within the work. This task is as much imposed on students of multi-media artefacts from popular and minority cultures as on those studying élite multi-media works produced by the dominant culture.

DICKENS AND PHIZ

All this may seem a long way from the question of illustrations for novels. I turn now to an example of that, the etchings on steel by 'Phiz' (Hablôt K. Browne) for Charles Dickens's *The Pickwick Papers*. The example is midway between popular and élite literature, neither quite one nor the other. The illustrations for *The Pickwick Papers* would seem to have little to do with the drama of the appearance and disappearance of the sun, its rising from the earth and setting in it, or with the 'Erscheinung' of Nature, *phusis*. Most of Phiz's plates show indoor scenes warmed by fires and lit by artificial means. Even those that are outdoor scenes or landscapes represent a fully humanized space centred on the activities of Pickwick and his friends. Neither nature in itself nor man's relation to nature is an important topic for either Dickens or Phiz. The most authoritative studies of Phiz's illustrations for *The Pickwick Papers*, works by Albert Johannsen, Robert Patten and Michael Steig,[78] stress Phiz's relative independence from Dickens and the way he worked in a separate iconographic or emblematic tradition, the tradition of Hogarth, Rowlandson, Cruikshank and others. But both Patten and Steig affirm the relative harmony of Phiz's plates and Dickens's text. The plates, as Steig puts it, 'provid[e] a running commentary, in visual language, upon the verbal text' (p. 34), or, as the dust-jacket of Steig's book puts it, 'a running visual gloss on the texts themselves, an iconographic counter-text that does not decorate the written text in a servile fashion but comments on it'. There would seem relatively little possibility for exploring the notion of an irreconcilable doubleness of text and picture through the example of *The Pickwick Papers*.

Nevertheless, a solar drama, involving a doubling of the sun, is, somewhat surprisingly, enacted in *The Pickwick Papers*. Steven Marcus, in a brilliant essay, has observed that the opening sentence of the novel is a parody of Genesis.[79] *The Pickwick Papers* enacts a creation myth, the birth of light and order out of chaotic darkness. The *fiat lux!* in this case is the appearance of a human 'logos', Dickens's all-creative narrating word that burst on the English-reading world with the invention of Pickwick. This creating energy continued to flow through novel after novel. As Dickens said, with sublime simplicity, 'I thought of Mr Pickwick, and wrote the first number'.[80] The first sentence of that first number of *The Pickwick Papers* does more than affirm a correspondence between the light-making word of God and the creative word of the novelist who makes characters out of nothing and brings into the light an entire fictional world. It signals the way this world enters with determining force into the culture of Dickens's readers and even, in time, into the culture of those who have not read Dickens. This is a good example of that inaugurating, culture-making power of the work of art I have proposed as an assumption for cultural studies. The reader will remember the law Henry James formulates whereby a novel should always be seen as 'putting forward illustrative claims (that is producing an effective illustration) by its own intrinsic virtue'.[81] This bringing to light, in the literal sense of 'illustration', always initially takes place in a novel by way of the written word, not by way of visual image, nor by way of pure thought. Dickens 'thought of Mr Pickwick', but Pickwick only came into the light of day when Dickens wrote down the first number.

If Pickwick comes into existence as language, this raises immediately a question of style. The first sentence of *The Pickwick Papers* presents itself in a language of ironic parody and transforms Dickens into Boz. Boz is then turned into the editor of 'papers' that he has not written but merely presents, after careful editorial scrutiny, to the reader. *The Pickwick Papers* consists of documents about documents. The reader searches in vain, in the *The Pickwick Papers*, for examples of a style that is without irony or parodic elements. Such a style would be 'sincere' and straightforward, the direct expression of the mind of the one who speaks, just as the *logos* (in the sense of 'mind') of God expresses itself in the *Logos* (in the sense of the Word, Christ). The second person of the Trinity mirrors the first exactly and without irony or figure. Dickens's making, however, is a mimic creation. It is fictional through and through, undermined by irony. It is a simulacrum, not a representation. Dickens's voice is a mock sun doubling the real one. Therefore it is always condemned to dwell in parody, in various forms of displacement and indirection. This is signalled in Dickens's taking the pseudonym 'Boz', as well as in the ostentatiously artificial polysyllabic style of the opening sentence of *The Pickwick Papers*. The creator of a fictional world is always condemned, from the outset, to write in a borrowed language. There is no 'straight' language in a mock creation illumined by a mock sun:

> The first ray of light which illumines the gloom, and converts into a dazzling brilliancy that obscurity in which the earlier history of the public career of the immortal Pickwick would appear to be involved, is derived from the perusal of the following entry in the Transactions of the Pickwick Club, which the editor of these papers feels the highest pleasure in laying before his readers, as a proof of the careful attention, indefatigable assiduity, and nice discrimination, with which his search among the multifarious documents confided to him has been conducted (p. 67).

This doubling of the real sun of God's creation by Dickens's mock creation of an illustrative language of narration, itself doubled and redoubled within itself in various forms of ironic parody, is dramatized within the novel in the consistent identification of Pickwick with a second sun. An example is the opening of the second chapter:

> That punctual servant of all work, the sun, had just risen, and begun to strike a light on the morning of the thirteenth of May, one thousand eight hundred and twenty-seven, when Mr Samuel Pickwick burst like another sun from his slumbers, threw open his chamber window, and looked out upon the world beneath (pp. 72–3).

The real sun is here humanized, diminished. This is effected both by the circumstantiality of the date, which incorporates the sun into the thoroughly man-made world of calendars, of counting and accounting, and by the figure that makes the sun not a divinity, Apollo, god of light, but no more than a servant who gets up before anyone else to strike a light. The sun plays Sam Weller to Mr Pickwick. The latter seems to have more of the characteristics of the 'real' sovereign sun, as he bursts from sleep and throws open the window.

Pickwick's characteristic activity is to leap out of bed like this each morning, ready to face whatever the new day will bring. As many critics of the novel have seen, *The Pickwick Papers* has an episodic structure. It follows the diurnal rhythm of the sun. The novel is, as Dickens himself said in the preface to the original edition of 1837, 'a mere series of adventures, in which the scenes are ever changing, and the characters come and go like the men and women we encounter in the real world' (p. 41). Dickens repeated this in the Announcement at the Conclusion of part Ten, composed while the novel was still being written and published. It was his intention, he said, to 'keep perpetually going on beginning again, regularly, until the end of the fair' (p. 903). These words too, it may be noted, are not Dickens's own, nor even those of the pseudonymous Boz, 'Mr Pickwick's Stage-Manager', as Dickens calls him in the Announcement (p. 902). The words are quoted from 'what the late eminent Mr John Richardson, of Horsemonger Lane Southwark, and the Yellow Caravan with the Brass Knocker, always said on behalf of himself and company, at the close of every performance' (p. 902). This citation works, like the reference within the novel to the Bath coach proprietor named Moses Pickwick, both to ground the novel in extra-fictional circumstantial reality and to hide Dickens's own voice behind a series of voices within voices. These voices are different ways of speaking and writing that are always assumed, in a complex act of ventriloquism. In the narrative proper, Pickwick, with his shining spectacles and beaming face, is a human sun inexhaustibly radiating benevolence, love and confidence in human goodness in a world that progressively becomes darker as the novel continues, more bereft of the real sun, and perhaps also bereft of that divine Providence for which the real sun traditionally stands: 'his countenance beamed with the most sunny smiles, laughter played round his lips, and good-humoured merriment twinkled in his eye' (p. 337). Even the warmest scenes in the novel, such as the description of Christmas at Dingley Dell, tend to be interiors enclosing a small group of happy friends and cutting them off from the threatening and unfriendly world outside. Pickwick is the centre of this enclosed world of human goodness, as in the description of him at the end of the novel:

> And in the midst of all this, stood Mr Pickwick, his counten-ance lighted up with smiles, which the heart of no man, woman, or child, could resist: himself the happiest of the group: shaking hands over and over again with the same people, and when his own hands were not so employed, rubbing them with pleasure: turning round in a different direction at every fresh expression of gratification or curi-osity, and inspiring everybody with his looks of gladness and delight.
>
> . . . There are dark shadows on the earth, but its lights are stronger in the contrast. Some men, like bats or owls, have better eyes for the darkness than for the light. We, who have no such optical powers, are better pleased to take our last parting look at the visionary companions of many solitary hours, when the brief sunshine of the world is blazing full upon them (pp. 895–6).

The voice of Boz here almost becomes the voice of Dickens. The author speaks for once in his own straightforward lan-guage, a language without irony and without parody. In order to do this he must define Pickwick and his friends as fictional beings, 'visionary companions'. He sees them, in his 'parting look', from the perspective an author has toward the imaginary characters he has created.

Pickwick, on the other hand, within the fiction, radiates looks of gladness on all around him, shedding benevolence as the sun sheds light. The brief sunshine of the world, celeb-rated by Dickens or Boz, has its source in the human radiance of Pickwick's goodness and in its reflection back to him from the happy faces of his amicable community. The whole group together makes an island of brightness surrounded by the double darkness of treacherous selfishness in persons and pettifogging injustice in institutions such as the law. 'The brief sunshine of the world' in Dickens's phrase is neither the outdoor sun of nature nor the transcendent sun of the supernatural world, to both of which Dickens sometimes makes reference in passages involving the sun. Examples of this are Esther Summerson's vision (note her name!) of Ches-ney Wold, the Dedlocks' country estate, in *Bleak House*, when she finds out that Lady Dedlock is her mother, and the trial of Magwitch in *Great Expectations*. Both allude to the natural sun as the symbol of God's benevolent providence within the natural and human worlds. Pickwick, however, is a thoroughly humanized sun, at most an indirect mediator of divine goodness.

What do Phiz's illustrations add to this drama of the double sun? Other interpreters of Phiz's illustrations have observed that the meaning of the etchings depends on similarities in design from one plate to another. As Robert Patten has noted, the structure of *Mr Pickwick in the Pound* (illus. 22), with the innocent Pickwick in the centre being looked at by a circle of worldly-wise laughing faces, is repeated in the structure of *Mr Pickwick and Sam in the Attorneys' Office*, where the spectators are Dodson and Fogg's four clerks:

> All the four clerks, with countenances expressive of the utmost amusement, and with their heads thrust over the wooden screen, were minutely inspecting the figure and general appearance of the supposed trifler with female hearts, and disturber of female happiness (p. 346).

As Patten observes, this composition, with Pickwick in the centre, surrounded by a crowd of watching figures, is repeated in many other plates.[82] Michael Steig recapitulates Patten's argument, modifies it, and offers further examples, including the parallelism in theme and graphic composition between *The Valentine* (illus. 23) and *The Trial*, with Serjeant Buzfuz in the latter replacing Sam's father in the former.

Steig, moreover, in *Dickens and Phiz*, has shown how to 'read' Phiz's illustrations, namely by a combination of interpretation of compositional features with interpretation of iconographic details that work, in the Hogarthian way, as the graphic representation of tropes: pun, metaphor and allegorical emblem. Examples noted by Steig are the stuffed owl in *Mrs Bardell Faints in Mr Pickwick's Arms*, the kitten attacking the remains of a meat pie in *Job Trotter Encounters Sam in Mr Muzzle's Kitchen*, or the spider's web in *The First Interview with Mr Serjeant Snubbin*, into which flies were introduced in the duplicate steel. All these details are Phiz's invention, with no literal basis in Dickens's text.[83] They make the relation between Phiz's illustrations and Dickens's novel not so much that of text and 'elucidating' commentary, to use Steig's word,

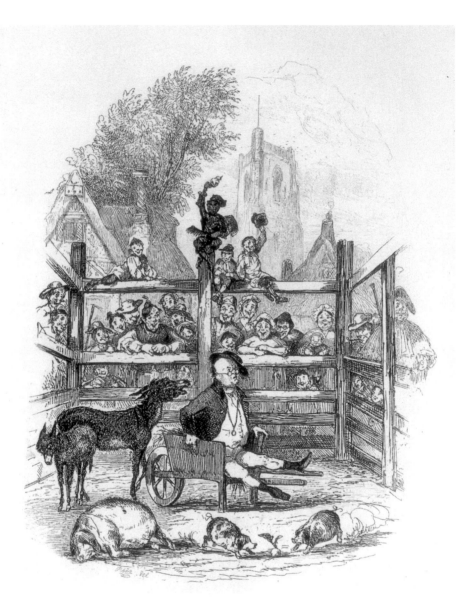

as that of two parallel, and to some degree incompatible, expressions with somewhat different traditions as controls on meaning, one in the form of the printed word, the other in the graphic form of impressions drawn from the etched steel. The relation between Phiz's etchings and Dickens's novel is a good example of the way an illustration for a novel always adds something more, something not in the text. The illustration, therefore, to some degree interferes with the text, as

22 'Phiz', *Mr Pickwick in the Pound*, from *The Pickwick Papers*, 1837.

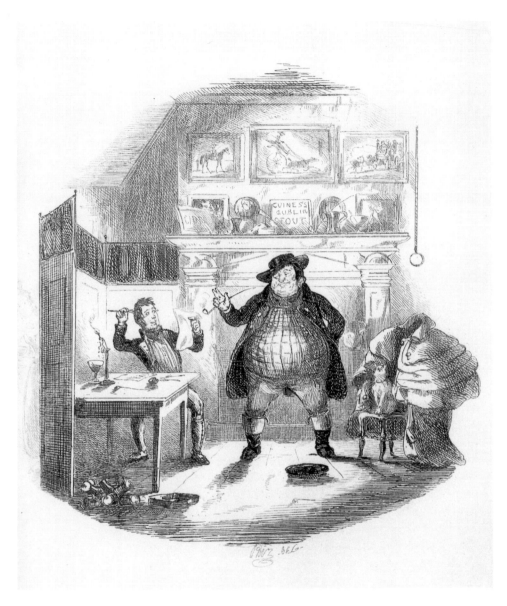

23 'Phiz', *The
Valentine*, from
*The Pickwick
Papers*, 1837.

two melodies playing simultaneously sometimes harmonize
and sometimes do not seem to go together. Mallarmé and
James were right to fear the independent power of illustration, the power so strongly affirmed in Phiz's plates.

Neither Patten nor Steig, nor anyone else to my knowledge,
has said anything about the most striking way Phiz's illustrations pick up something from Dickens's text and do something purely graphic with it. If Pickwick's beaming face and

shining spectacles make him, in Dickens's words, 'another sun', and if he is repeatedly called 'the illustrious Pickwick',[84] Phiz displaces that doubling once more from Pickwick's round head to his round stomach. In plate after plate Pickwick's globular white stomach, with the tiny circle of his gold watch on its chain as focus, not only commands the centre of the composition, but functions as a secondary source of illumination. Light seems to radiate in all directions from Pickwick's stomach to bring into visibility objects and people in what are often dark and enclosed interiors. Phiz was justified in what he does with Pickwick's body by what Boz says in the first chapter, citing the notes of the Secretary of the Pickwick Club, about Pickwick's

> tights and gaiters, which, had they clothed an ordinary man, might have passed without observation, but which, when Pickwick clothed them – if we may use the expression – inspired involuntary awe and respect (p. 69).

Pickwick does indeed clothe his tights and gaiters in Phiz's plates. His legs are drawn almost as the naked lower body of an older man, the absence or almost total absence of visible indications of his sex serving to make him look somewhat grossly epicene. This reminds the viewer that old age may return to childhood in this respect, just as Pickwick's innocence is childish. It also works to displace the sign of Pickwick's mature masculinity from what is not shown to that radiant, Falstaffian, abundantly protruding stomach that *is* shown.

Sometimes there is a natural light-source in these plates, a light coming in from outside. This sets the real sun against Pickwick's belly as counter-sun. Sometimes, when the scene is outdoors, Pickwick as second sun is set more directly against the real sun, though never with even so much direct representation of the latter as there is in Holbein's *The Last Furrow*, not to speak of the direct presence of the sun as the dazzling white centre of the vortex of coloured light in so many of Turner's paintings.

Pickwick's stomach is so often a compositional centre in Phiz's illustrations for *The Pickwick Papers* that those illustrations may almost be said to be a series of variations of that single graphic structure. In *Mr Pickwick in the Pound* (illus. 22),[85] the white Pickwickian stomach with its punctuating

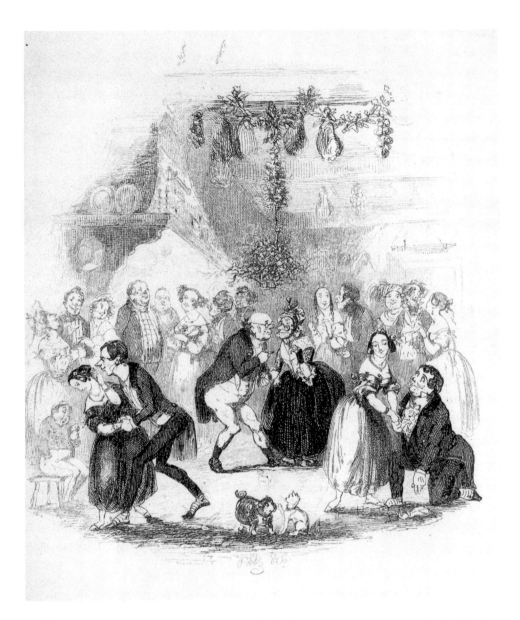

watch is the centre of the lower composition, encircled by the rooting piglets, the sleeping mother hog, the braying donkey and the double ring of mocking faces. This round enclosure is doubled by the round patch of sky and light above, centred, as in Holbein's *The Last Furrow*, on the tower of the village church, with whatever complexity of satiric and emblematic implication this may have. In *Christmas Eve at Mr Wardle's* (illus. 24), Pickwick's stomach is once more the centre of the composition, as he kisses the old lady under the mistletoe. The composition in this case is an X shape. Pickwick's stomach seems to be the source of light for the floor and for the dresses of the ladies around him, though that light-source is echoed by the fire at the upper middle-left and by the open door at the middle upper-right. In *Mr Pickwick Slides* (illus. 25), the cross made by Pickwick's four limbs reaches out toward the ring of spectators. Once more, Pickwick's stomach

25 'Phiz', *Mr Pickwick Slides*, from *The Pickwick Papers*, 1837.

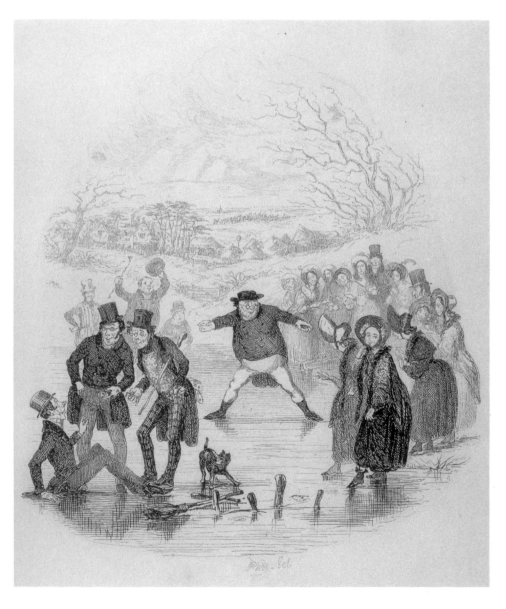

26 'Phiz', *Mr
Wardle and his
Friends Under the
Influence of the
Salmon*, from *The
Pickwick Papers*,
1837.

is in the centre, outlined as a full globe and doubled by an
upper region of open-lit sky, within which no globe of the
sun is visible. In *The Valentine* (illus. 23), the vast girth of Mr
Weller, senior, replaces Pickwick's stomach. Weller's belly is
outlined almost like a globe with lines of latitude and long-
itude. It seems to have the power to cast light on the floor
and on the screen behind Sam to the left, though the real
light-source is probably the fireplace that Mr Weller's huge

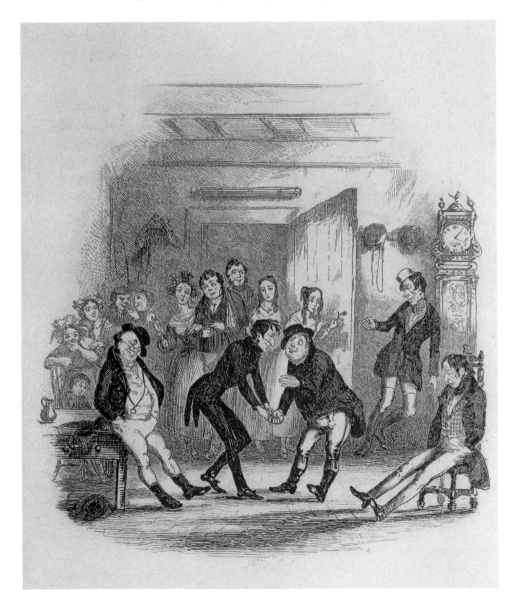

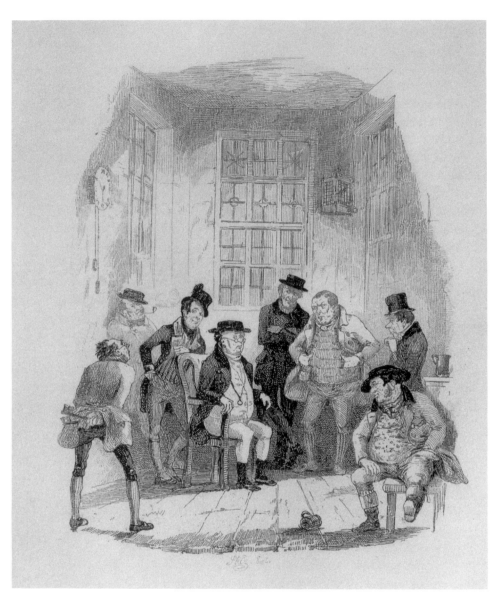

bulk obscures. In *Mr Wardle and his Friends Under the Influence of the Salmon*, in *The Card Room at Bath*, in *Mr Pickwick Sits for his Portrait* and in *Discovery of Jingle in the Fleet* (illus. 26–29), Phiz presents further variations on this basic composition, with its play of doubled and redoubled light centred on Pickwick's belly as solar metaphor. Of the relation of Phiz's *The Valentine* to the chapter it illustrates, and of the relation of that chapter itself, with its remarkable comments on figurative and

27 'Phiz', *Mr Pickwick Sits for his Portrait*, from *The Pickwick Papers*, 1837.

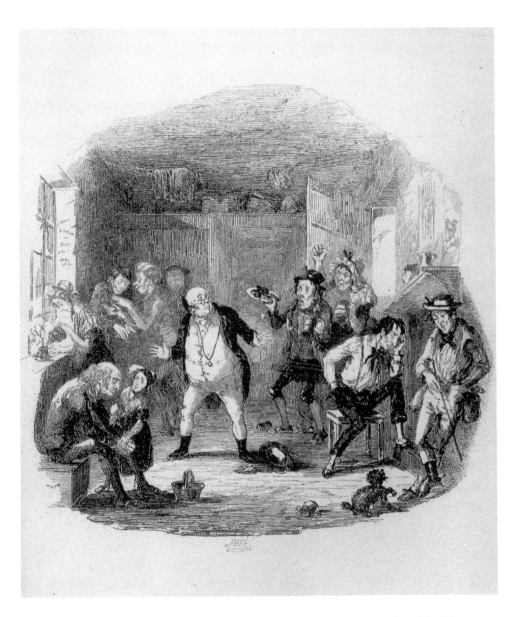

28 'Phiz',
*Discovery of Jingle
in the Fleet*, from
*The Pickwick
Papers*, 1837.

literal language, and on style generally, to *The Pickwick Papers*
as a whole there would be much to say, but I shall defer that
saying.

If Dickens in what he writes has Pickwick perform the role
of a second sun, Phiz in his illustrations for that writing has
doubled that doubling once more in a way that is another
indication that each sign, whether graphic or verbal, not only
illustrates in the end itself, but also is divided within itself,

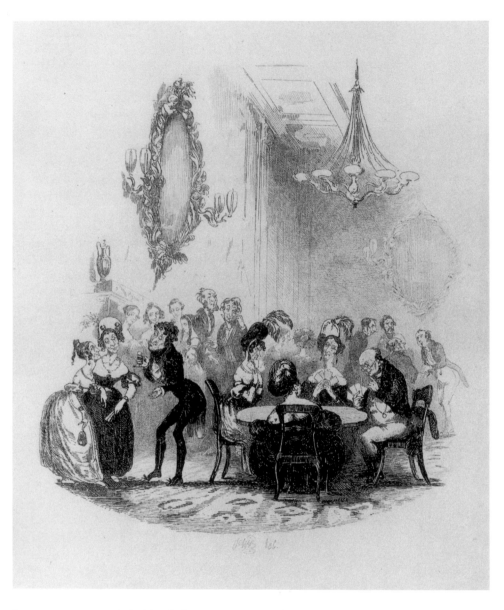

heterogeneous, inhabited by its own other. Each sign, whether graphic or verbal, brings something of its own into the light rather than copying, commenting on, or elucidating some other sign. Each sign is a separate sun. It brings its own light to light and irradiates everything from that new centre, as Pickwick's stomach (or Mr Weller's) does in Phiz's plates.

This structure – Pickwick with his beaming face as a second sun that is then redoubled by the focus on his shining white

29 'Phiz', *The Card Room at Bath*, from *The Pickwick Papers*, 1837.

stomach in Phiz's etchings – may be taken as an emblem of the relationship always involved in illustration, of which illustrations for novels are a special case. In all illustrations one doubling always invites further duplications, like one sun beside another in a diminishing row potentially *ad infinitum*. Even the first sun, that blazing ball in the sky, is already the second, since it is the appearance, or *Erscheinung*, of what it stands for, the first sun no-one can ever see. Wallace Stevens, modern master of the solar trajectory, calls that first sun 'the inconceivable idea of the sun'.[86] Any sun, real or graphic, is the illustration of the *first* first sun. The real sun, like any painting of the sun, is the sensible shining of the idea of the sun.

A triple doubling, doubling within the stylistic texture, doubling of the text by illustration, doubling within the illustrations themselves, manifests itself in the cases studied so far. The acerb irony of Mark Twain, his suspicion that words only artificially control an anarchy of contradictory potential meanings in a picture, may seem quite different from Dickens's confidence that his narrative can dominate the plates that illustrate it. Dickens's replacement of Cruikshank by Phiz, however, and the notorious care he took to dictate to Phiz what should be illustrated and even to make Phiz re-do unsatisfactory plates are evidence of a lurking uneasiness. The example of Phiz's plates for *The Pickwick Papers* demonstrates not only that Dickens was right to be uneasy, but that Phiz managed to get past Dickens's censorship a meaning that exceeds, and even to some degree subverts, Dickens's text. *The Pickwick Papers* rather supports than challenges Twain's insight. It would certainly not support the claims of an ideological, historical or national difference between Twain and Dickens.

TURNER

I turn now to J. M. W. Turner as my last illustration of the topic of illustration. Many of Turner's paintings, watercolours and sketches represent the sun as such, there on the canvas or paper, or represent its direct effects on the atmosphere. To make a full inventory of them would almost be to tell the whole story of Turner's work. One example out of many is *Sun Rising Through Vapour; Fishermen Cleaning and Selling Fish*, exhibited in 1807, now in the National Gallery in London (illus. 30). Nearly all Turner's critics from Ruskin on have had something to say about Turner's suns. A notable example is Ronald Paulson in his admirable essay, 'Turner's Graffiti: The Sun and Its Glosses'.[87] Paulson also gives a useful summary of all the things the sun meant in eighteenth-century poetry, painting, philosophy and politics. I shall build on these books and essays, especially on Paulson's essay, to focus on what Turner implies for the notion of illustration as such and for the relation of graphic to verbal forms of expression. My chief example is The 'Sun of Venice' Going to Sea (exh. 1843; illus. 43), but we need to see that painting in the context of large-scale recurrences of theme and composition that organize Turner's work as a whole.

Paulson sees a conflict between graphic and verbal forms in Turner's work, as well as between graphic and iconographic forms. He also sees a movement from primordial splashes or splotches of colour toward more verbal forms of articulation that suppress what is subversive, shocking or revolutionary in the original, purely graphic, appearance. That graphic manifestation remains sufficiently visible, nevertheless, even in the most literary, finished and representational of Turner's paintings, to have generated violent hostility to Turner's work as mere daubs of paint. This is abundantly documented in early reviews of his paintings. Moreover, the relation of graphic to verbal in Turner's work is by no means always that of the temporal priority of the former over the latter, nor is the graphic always the subversive, the verbal the rationalizing or repressive.

Many of Turner's most celebrated paintings are illustrations of pre-existing verbal documents. An example is Ulysses Deriding Polyphemus (exh. 1829; illus. 31, 32). That painting, even though it may have begun as a non-literary seascape and shorescape, illustrates a passage in the Odyssey, just as the two Dido paintings illustrate the Aeneid. Regulus (1828, reworked 1837; illus. 33) follows the verbal sources for the story of Regulus, for example a passage in Horace. The painting perhaps even follows the poem on Regulus Turner inscribed in his verse book, though the poem may follow the painting. The Angel Standing in the Sun (exh. 1846; illus. 41) not only illustrates the avenging Angel of the Book of Revelation and the Angel of Darkness in Samuel Rogers's poem

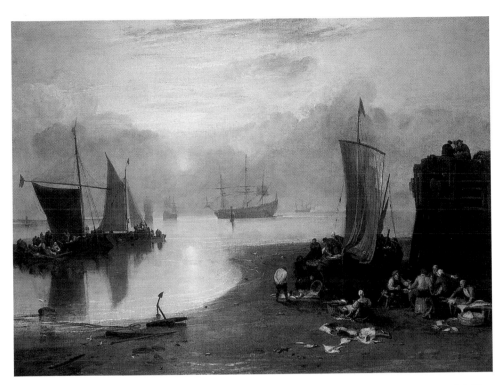

30 J.M.W. Turner, *Sun Rising Through Vapour; Fishermen Cleaning and Selling Fish*, 1807.

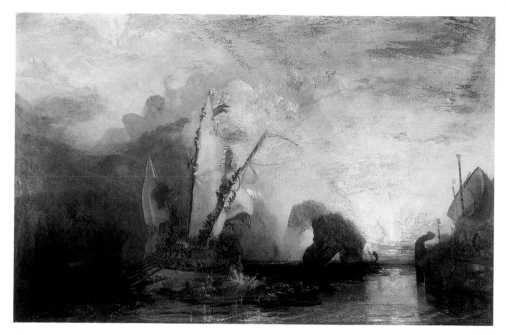

above: 31 J.M.W. Turner, *Ulysses Deriding Polyphemus*, 1829.

opposite: 32 Detail of illus. 31.

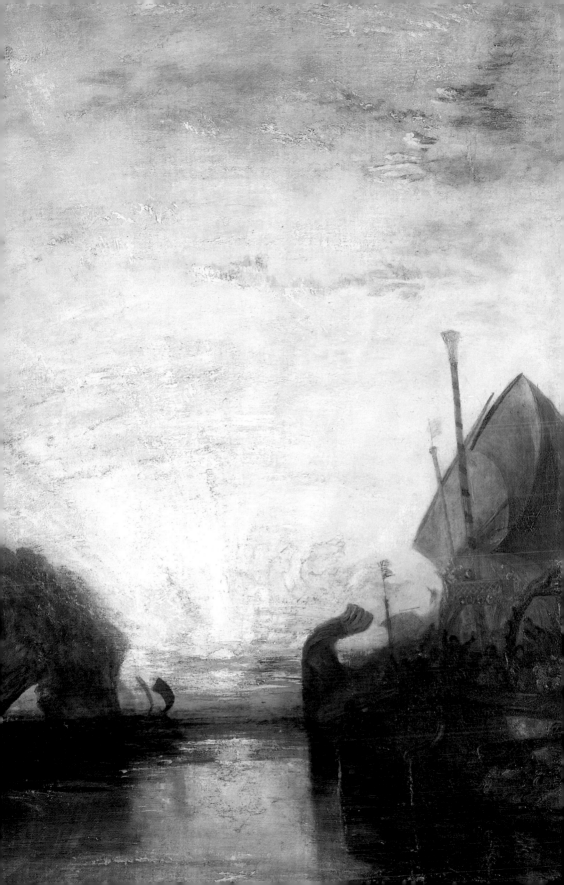

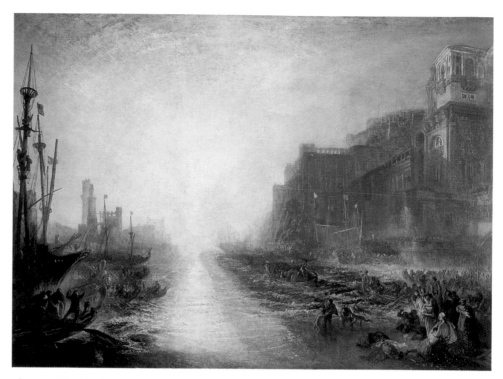

above: 33 J.M.W. Turner, *Regulus,* 1828, reworked 1837.

opposite: 34 Detail of illus. 33.

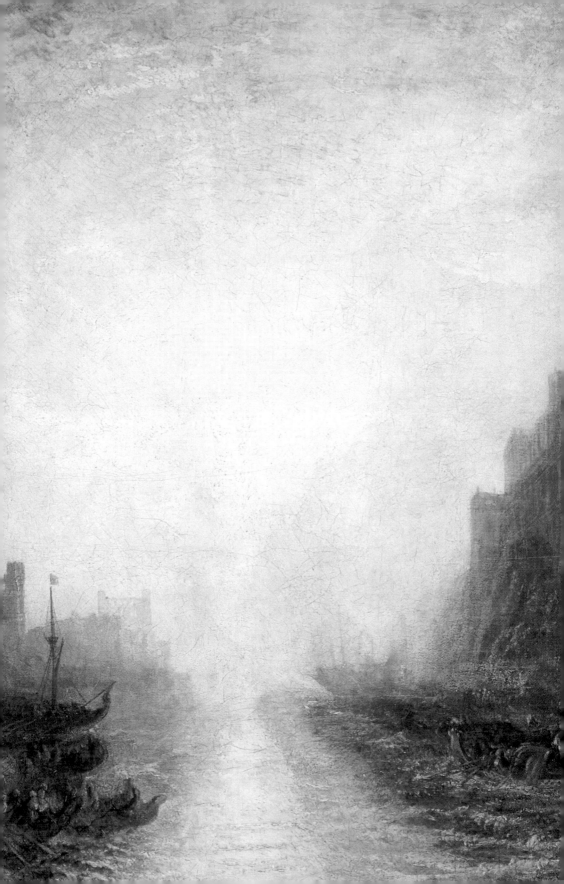

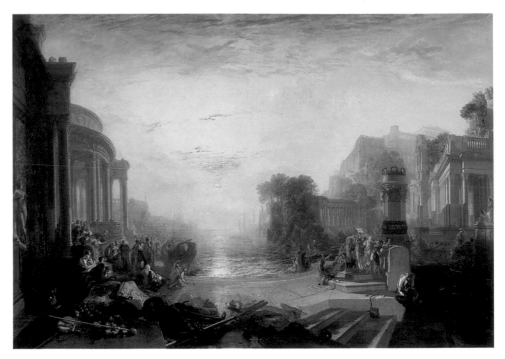

above: 35 J.M.W. Turner, *The Decline of the Carthaginian Empire*, 1817.

opposite: 36 Detail of illus. 35.

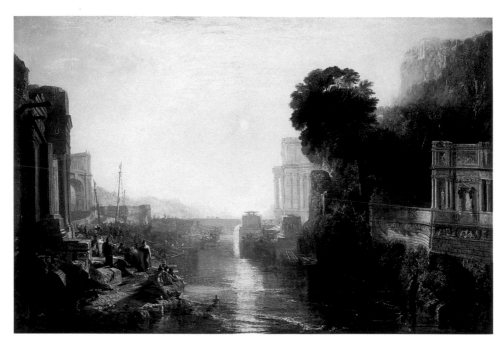

37 J.M.W. Turner, *Dido Building Carthage*, 1815.

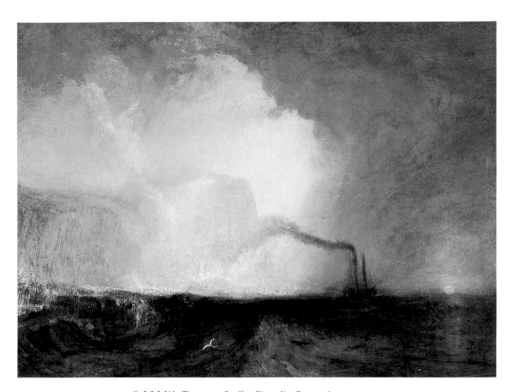

38 J.M.W. Turner, *Staffa, Fingal's Cave*, 1832.

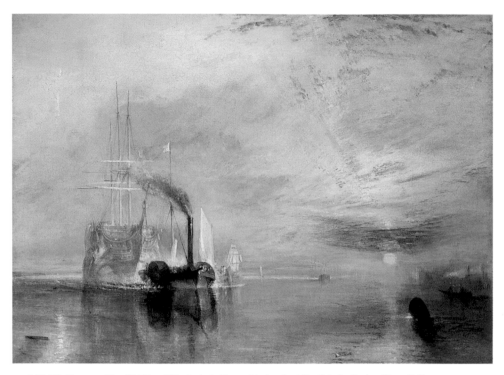

39 J.M.W. Turner, *The Fighting 'Téméraire', Tugged to her Last Berth to be Broken Up*, 1838.

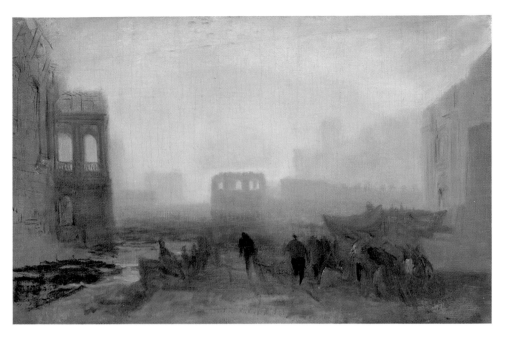

40 J.M.W. Turner, *Claudian Harbour Scene, c.* 1828.

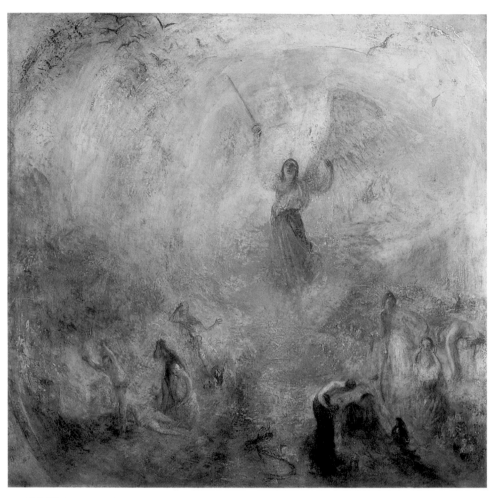

41 J.M.W. Turner, *The Angel Standing in the Sun*, 1846.

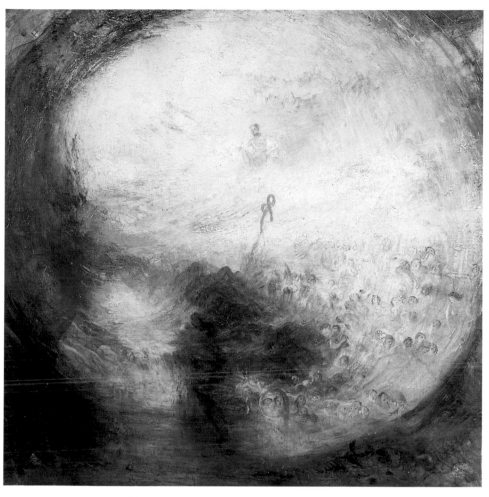

42 J.M.W. Turner, *Light and Colour (Goethe's Theory) – the Morning after the Deluge – Moses Writing the Book of Genesis*, 1843.

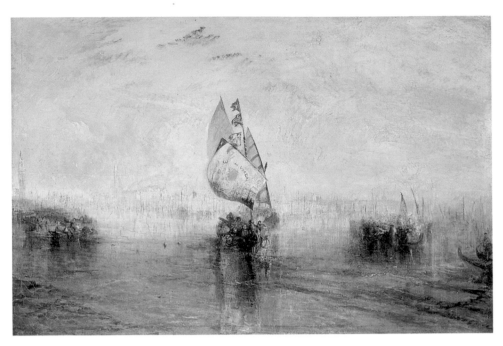

above: 43 J.M.W. Turner, *The 'Sun of Venice' Going to Sea,* 1843.

opposite: 44 Detail of illus. 43.

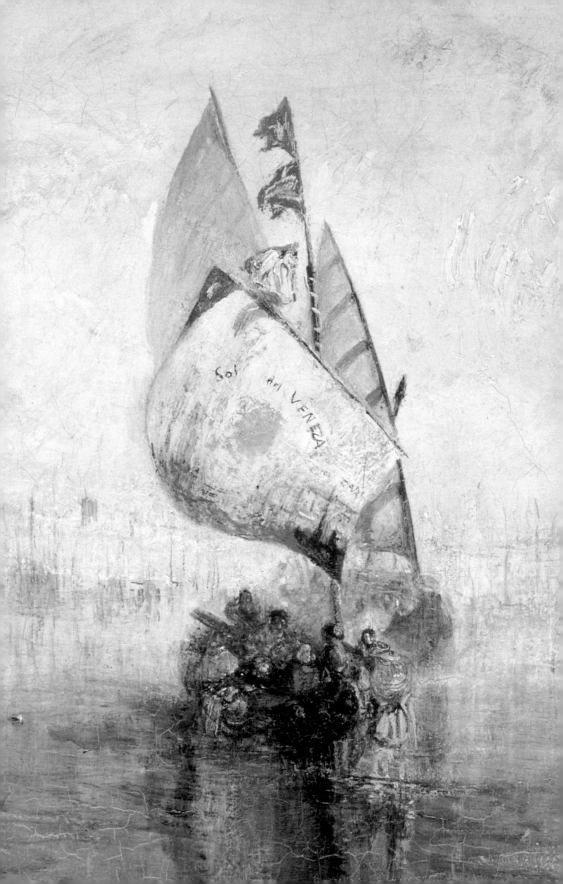

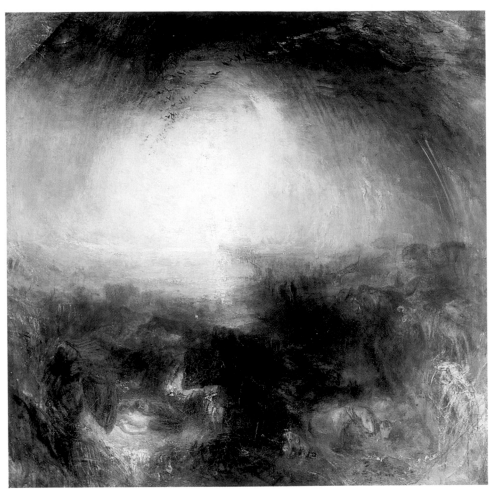

45 J.M.W. Turner, *Shade and Darkness – the Evening of the Deluge*, 1843.

The Voyage of Columbus. It also illustrates Ruskin's description in *Modern Painters* (1843) of Turner 'standing like the great angel of the Apocalypse, clothed with a cloud, with a rainbow upon his head, and with the sun and stars given into his hand' (*Works*, III, p. 254). Even two of the purest experiments in colour, *Shade and Darkness – the Evening of the Deluge.* (exh. 1843; illus. 45) and *Light and Colour (Goethe's Theory) – the Morning after the Deluge – Moses Writing the Book of Genesis* (exh. 1843; illus. 42), are, after all, pictures of scenes in the Bible. They are also illustrations of Goethe's *Zur Farbenlehre* (translated as *The Theory of Colour*). Nor are these pre-existing verbal expressions necessarily less primordial or less subversive than the paintings.

The description in the *Odyssey* of the blinding of Polyphemus by Odysseus and his men with a sharpened and heated olive stick, for example, is powerful and disturbing.[88] The passage is a figure for a hideous sexual penetration and at the same time describes a displaced act of castration, the unmanning of the Cyclops by blinding him. Could it be that Turner saw a figure for his own name and his own equivocal power in the two figures for turning Homer uses, the turning of the shipwright's drill and the wringing of the white-hot metal when it is plunged in water by the smith? Turner's painting (illus. 31) illustrates not the blinding of Polyphemus but the later scene when Ulysses and his men have returned safely to their ship. Ulysses taunts Polyphemus when the latter tries to find out the name of the man who has blinded him. When he gets the Cyclops drunk Ulysses says his name is 'Nohbdy', as Fitzgerald translates it, but after he has blinded Polyphemus and returned to his ship, he has the temerity to shout out his real name. Now that Polyphemus knows Ulysses's name he has power over him and can call on Poseidon to curse him: 'Let him lose all companions, and return / under strange sail to bitter days at home' (Fitzgerald trans., IX, 161). Ulysses, among his other epithets, is called 'πολύτροπο' (*polytropo*) in the first line of the *Odyssey*, 'resourceful', 'wily', 'versatile', most literally 'a man of many turns'.[89] This is another turn of phrase for turning, and so perhaps another punning trope connecting Turner and Ulysses. The passages in the *Odyssey* are presupposed in Turner's painting and confirm its import. This parallels the way the *Regulus* may be seen as placing the spectator in the position of Regulus with his eyelids cut off about to be blinded by the sun only if we already know the story of Regulus in its verbal forms. That story in turn can hardly be said to be a suppression of the dangerous power of the sun or of the temerity involved in challenging it by looking it in the eye. Paulson's hypothesis of a suppression of the revolutionary graphic by the civilized verbal must be replaced by the concept of a complex translation back and forth from one to the other.

TURNER'S DOUBLINGS

Far from being a smooth movement from subversive graphic to repressive verbal, the interaction between graphic and verbal in Turner is a reciprocal relation in which sometimes one is prior, sometimes the other. Each may bring out disturbing elements the other hides. Those elements are a certain version of the sun's trajectory. The outlines of that narrative may be discerned in a comparative reading of the many paintings by Turner that have a common composition and tell one version or another of the same troubling story. This composition centres on the sun rising or setting in sovereign splendour there in the sky. The sun in Turner's paintings is the focus of a violent vortex of swirling light spiralling out from a white-hot centre toward all the colours, the hot reds, oranges and yellows, then the cooler greens and blues, all the way out to black, total absence of colour. Turner's sun usually hangs over some abyss or fissure: a river, canal, harbour or lake, a valley, a chasm in the Alps, or, most often, simply the profound depths of the sea.

Turner's sea is sometimes beguilingly flat, calm and translucent, as in *Ulysses Deriding Polyphemus* (illus. 31) or *The 'Sun of Venice' Going to Sea* (illus. 44). But in many of Turner's splendid seapieces the sea is in violent turmoil. In either case it is always a profound depth waiting to swallow up whatever is on its surface. Into this chasm the sun disappears each day, to rise again each morning in its diurnal course, as the sun is rising in *Dido Building Carthage* (exh. 1815; illus. 37), but setting as a golden afternoon glow in *The Decline of the Carthaginian Empire* (exh. 1817; illus. 35, 36). It is difficult, in Turner's paintings of the sun in proximity to the horizon, to tell whether the sun is rising or setting, unless a clue is given by some external verbal evidence in the title of the painting, in verses appended to it in the catalogue, or through recognition of the geographic location. If Turner had not said so, the spectator would not know whether the sun is rising or setting through vapour, any more than she or he would know, without the title, the exact relation of Lee and Jackson in that painting Mark Twain mocks (illus. 14).

Another element, however, is characteristically present in Turner's compositions. Usually to the left, sometimes to the right, there is often another channel of light, or another focus of attention: a pier, a ship, a group of people, a mountain. Quite often this subsidiary focus involves some secondary light-source, made by human beings or signifying them. This light is a mock human sun, usually emanating with a red glow from the earth or from some human enclosure like a ship or a building. This second source of light is Turner's version of the theme of the second sun. Such paintings have a doubled luminous foyer. Charles Stuckey has investigated this theme in *Temporal Imagery in the Early Romantic Landscape*.[90] The image or idea of multiple suns is uncanny and disturbing, as in the passage from Xenophanes cited in reference 41, or as in a dream I once had of a horizontal row of suns, diminishing in brightness, lined up along the horizon.

The second light-source, with its human group, represents in Turner's paintings humankind's defiant challenge to the sun, the making of a second sun, a Promethean stealing of fire. In *Newark Abbey on the Wey* (exh. 1807?) the second light-source is the red glow of the cosy fire in the lighter tied up to the dock on the right of the picture. In *Ulysses Deriding Polyphemus* (illus. 31), the second foyer of light is the red volcanic glow in the lower left of the canvas, presumably the fire in Polyphemus's cave. The red glow recalls, as one critic has noted, the volcanic glow of such a Mediterranean island as Stromboli. In another painting, *Staffa, Fingal's Cave* (exh. 1832; illus. 38), the lurid sun, orange and yellow, on the right is overshadowed by the great swirl of white, yellow and greenish-grey to the left, where the shore is located. The sun in this painting is doubled by the tiny dots of orange on the side of the steamboat – sidelights or a fire in its boiler. The configuration of the waves gives the painting a binocular composition. A great circle on the right centred on the sun is matched by another much brighter circle on the left centred on the cliffs. In the two Carthaginian paintings the sun rising or setting is opposed to the human groups, Dido planning Carthage with her architects in one case and the Carthaginians in their decadence and lassitude in the other (illus. 35, 37). Taken together the two paintings say that what goes up must come down. Those who imitate the sun in its constructive power must also in the end imitate it in its setting and disappearance. The decline of Carthage is a proleptic warning of the decline of Rome. The echo of Gibbon's title in the title *The Decline of the Carthaginian Empire* confirms this. As W. J. T. Mitchell has suggested, there is also a contemporary warning and political import directed against Britain's growing imperial hopes in the first half of the nineteenth century, as westward the course of empire took its way. Even though the Victorians were to boast that 'the sun never sets on the British Empire', sooner or later even that new empire was to disappear. The sun tells you what will happen if you become like the sun. In the end you will sink and vanish.

In *The Fighting 'Téméraire', Tugged to her Last Berth to be Broken Up* (exh. 1839; illus. 39), to give a last example, the second source of light and energy is the red fire on the deck and the red in the smoke from the stack in the steam-tug to the left. This painting is another version of Turner's drama of the imitation of the sun. The brave ship must, in the end, vanish as the sun vanishes every day. The *Téméraire* is being tugged to be broken up in a line that will converge with the line of light extending straight downward from the sun into the depths of the sea. According to a powerful emblematic tradition, as Stephen Bann has reminded me, all these ships in Turner's paintings are not only representational but also part of a moral, political and metaphysical allegory.

The story Turner's paintings tell is almost always presented from a male perspective. In that story, any man who puts himself in the place of the sun, who challenges the sun, or doubles it, is in a double bind. On the one hand, this act of temerity may be punished by the sun, as the one who looks the sun in the eye is blinded, as Regulus is blinded, or as Polyphemus is blinded, or as an aspiring son may be defeated by his father and so fail to replace the father in masculine sovereignty, in a reversal of the Oedipal narrative. In *Ulysses Deriding Polyphemus*, Polyphemus is the challenger of the sun, the Promethean stealer of fire, and Ulysses – the son whose fortune is rising – is an agent of the avenging, blinding, emasculating sun. On the other hand, if the aspiring human figure succeeds in doubling the sun, if he takes on the sun's role and becomes a source of power, light and masculine authority, then he is destined also to enact the full course of the sun's trajectory. He will vanish, as the sun does every day, into the chasm of death that, sooner or later, swallows up all figures of history and legend.

The dangerous imitation of the sun is given in Turner's work broad scope as a general interpretation, from a masculine perspective, of human life in history and in myth. Ronald Paulson is right, however, to say that all these stories are also, in one way or another, emblems of the special way Turner himself enacted in his own work the drama of the double sun. In certain of his paintings this theme appears with special clarity. To these I now turn.

TURNER AS SECOND SUN

The elements of Turner's story of the artist as second sun or as sun-maker are easy to trace. In the well-known description of Turner reworking the *Regulus* (illus. 33) at the British Institution for its exhibition there in 1837 (it was first shown in Rome in 1828–9), the artist labours with ferocious energy to shape a model of the sun on the canvas out of thick gobs of paint (illus. 34). Here is the description of Turner making a sun:

> He was absorbed in his work, did not look about him, but kept on scumbling a lot of white into his picture – nearly all over it . . . The picture was a mass of red and yellow of all varieties. Every object was in this fiery state. He had a large palette, nothing in it but a huge lump of flake-white; he had two or three biggish hog tools to work with, and with these he was driving the white into all the hollows, and every part of the surface. This was the only work he did, and it was the finishing stroke. The sun, as I have said, was in the centre; from it were drawn – ruled – lines to mark the rays; these lines were rather strongly marked, I suppose to guide his eye. The picture gradually became wonderfully effective, just the effect of brilliant sunlight

absorbing everything and throwing a misty haze over every object. Standing sideway of the canvas, I saw that the sun was a lump of white standing out like the boss on a shield.[91]

An early critic said that the sun in this painting 'absolutely dazzles the eyes',[92] and another said, 'the only way to be reconciled to the picture is to look at it from as great a distance as the width of the gallery will allow of, and then you see nothing but a burst of sunlight'.[93] These early critics recognized some obscure danger involved in looking at this picture. It is like looking the sun in the eye. There is danger of being blinded. Best is to look at a safe distance, from the other side of the room.[94]

The oil sketch, probably of 1828, in the Tate Gallery, entitled *Claudian Harbour Scene* (illus. 40) may be a preliminary version of *Regulus*. The *Claudian Harbour Scene* may show Regulus as a hooded figure to the right being led out to be blinded by the sun or perhaps surrounded by his family and friends in Rome about to embark for his voyage back to certain death in Carthage. Andrew Wilton, following Ruskin, has argued that the *Regulus* itself presents the latter scene. It has, he says, the pomp and formality of a traditional embarkation scene rather than the more sordid atmosphere of a public torturing. The painting was entitled *Regulus* during the nineteenth century. Wilton adduces as support of his interpretation an engraving made in 1840 that shows Regulus as one of a crowd of figures descending steps to the right.[95] John Gage, on the other hand, argues that the scene is Carthage and that the absence in the *Regulus* of 1837 of any figure identifiable as Regulus means that the viewer of the painting is placed in the position of Regulus at the moment before he is blinded. Regulus is seeing the world for the last time. He sees to the left the spiked barrel in which he is to be killed after being blinded.[96] The historical Regulus, Roman general and Consul, was punished by the Carthaginians, whose prisoner he was, for having failed to negotiate an exchange of prisoners between the Romans and the Carthaginians. His eyelids were cut off and then he was exposed to the sun, thereby blinded. He was given the *coup de grâce* by being rolled in a spiked barrel.

On either interpretation of its locale and action the central meaning of the painting must be the same. If the scene is

Rome, the painting shows Regulus's heroically nonchalant farewell to his family and friends.[97] The barrel on the left and the blazing sun that dazzles the spectator's eye are surely proleptic of Regulus's fate. Moreover, the similarity between the harbour scene in the *Regulus* and those in *Dido Building Carthage* (illus. 37) and *The Decline of the Carthaginian Empire* (illus. 35) make Rome the double of Carthage and reinforce the proleptic force of the painting. If John Gage's reading is correct, then the scene is Carthage, and the more melodramatic reading of the painting as deliberately placing the viewer in the position of Regulus the moment before he is blinded is justified. Even if Wilton is right, the painted sun is still a warning to those who challenge it. In either case, the painting represents, more forcefully than any other by Turner, the blinding power of the sun and, indirectly, the dangerous power of the painter who makes out of pigment a replica of the sun. Turner's *Regulus* is an extraordinary emblem of this painter's claim to be able to create a mock sun, a replica that will have the same terrible power over the man who dares look at it as the real sun does.[98] Turner's project as a painter was to create out of paint a second sun that would be not an imitation of light, but a light-source itself. Turner wanted to make of earthly materials that produce colour by reflection an equivalent in power of the aerial colours made by the prismatic splitting of pure white light.

GOETHE

Here, understanding Turner's colour theory and its analogy with Goethe's *Zur Farbenlehre* is essential to the interpretation of Turner's work. All three of the elements in this relation are complex and problematic: Turner's theory of colours in itself; Goethe's theory of colours in itself;[99] the influence of the latter on the former; the harmony or disharmony between them. Only the sketch-map of a direction to follow will be given here in illustration of what a full illumination of this terrain might be.

Exactly what are we to make of two strange paintings by Turner: *Shade and Darkness – the Evening of the Deluge* (illus. 45) and *Light and Colour (Goethe's Theory) – the Morning after the Deluge* (illus. 42)? The paintings were exhibited in 1843, three years after Turner's friend Sir Charles Eastlake published his translation of Goethe's *Zur Farbenlehre*. The paintings represent the most apocalyptic version of Turner's basic myth: the drowning of the whole living world in the primal Flood, everything vanishing as the sun sets on that evening of the Deluge. As the sun sets, the colours of what is visible move through what Goethe called the 'minus', or cold, colours of blue-green, blue and purple toward black, total absence of light. The next morning, the sun rises again. With it appear again the warm, or 'plus', colours: red, yellow and orange. As other critics have noted, however,[100] there are plus colours present in *Evening* and minus colours in *Morning*. The opposition seems rather to be between material colours on the one hand, that bring darkness, and aerial colours, on the other, the embodiment of light. Far from reaffirming Goethe's theory that colour is an intrinsic manifestation of the nature of material things rather than the result of a Newtonian splitting of light, Turner, according to Gowing, Heffernan and Jack Lindsay,[101] believed that colours come wholly from light, whereas matter is the privation of light and colour.

Matters are not quite so categorical here, however. In his first Academy lecture in the series of 1818, Turner rejected the mixing of pigments in painting in favour of placing side by side pure pigments that would be blended by the eye to produce by reflection an effect of aerial colour:

> [If] we mix two, we reduce the purity of the first a third impairs that purity still more and all beyond is minotony [sic], discord, and mud . . . White in Prismatic order as Daylight is the union or compound [of] Light while the Commixture of our material *colours* becomes the opposite that [is] the destruction of all or in other words – Darkness. Light is therefore colour, and shadow the privation of it by the Removal of these rays of colour or subduction of power and throughout nature these [?rays] are to be found in the ruling principles of diurnal variations, the gray dawn, the yellow morning.
> golden sun rise and red departing ray, in ever changing combination; these are the pure combinations [of] Aerial colours.[102]

However, as Heffernan observes, 'Turner's problem was to find a way of representing these pure combinations of aerial colour with material pigments' (p. 142). The way to do this,

Turner found, is to place on the canvas pure material colours that will reflect to the eye something like the colours of aerial light. This was his theory of 'optical fusion'. Even mixing two colours moves the painting toward mud. Only unmixed colours on the canvas will keep shadow out. Not material colours themselves but their 'commixture' is 'shadow' or 'darkness'. An example of this use of pure unmixed colours is the description of Turner finishing the *Regulus* with nothing on his palette but 'a huge lump of flake-white'. If the real sun and its rays of yellow, gold and red are pure white light divided, the suns and colours on Turner's canvases are representations, emblems, tropes of the sun and what it shines on. These representations are made of material pigment, pure colours set side by side to be fused by the eye to make a new colour that mimes effects of aerial light. Heffernan's example of this is the way in Turner's *Light and Colour (Goethe's Theory) – the Morning after the Deluge* (illus. 42) 'strands of red, yellow, and orange emanate from a massive sun of light, but here also they are juxtaposed for the eye to fuse them' (p. 143).

Turner's confidence in the representational power of his paintings, their ability to substitute for the sun's power, may be compared to Goethe's reservations about the coloured plates used as illustration in his *Zur Farbenlehre*. Of the latter, Goethe says:

> The plates which generally accompany works like the present are thus a most inadequate substitute for all this [an 'exhibition' in which 'Nature herself (is) present to the reader']; a physical phenomenon exhibiting its effects on all sides is not to be arrested in lines nor denoted by a section . . . In many cases, however, such diagrams represent mere notions [*nur Begriffe*]; they are symbolical resources, hieroglyphic modes of communication [*es sind symbolische Hülfsmittel, hieroglyphische Überlieferungsweisen*], which by degrees assume the place of the phenomena and of Nature herself, and thus rather hinder than promote true knowledge.[103]

Goethe's theory of colours is dialectical. It is the intersection, conflict, interaction and possible sublation of two theories of the sign. Goethe distinguishes three kinds of colour: physiological colour belonging to the eye ('dem Auge angehören'); 'physical' or aerial colour brought into visibility in some colourless medium; 'chemical' colour belonging intrinsically to the object ('den Gegenständen angehörig') and manifesting its essence in its vitality, its share in the universal life of Nature (E, lv; G, 325). For Goethe, the realm of colours is a text to be read. It is a set of signs to be interpreted, like the realms of sound, taste and feeling presented to the other senses. Colours of all three sorts are tropes of one kind or another – metaphors, synecdoches, metonymies, personifications, ironies, catachreses – of an unknown X Goethe calls Nature ('die Natur'). Nature in itself is 'the ungraspable' ('das Unerforschliche').[104] In all its manifestations of itself, for example in the world of colours, Nature may be indirectly grasped, as we grasp the literal by way of a figure. In the preface to the first edition of *Zur Farbenlehre*, Goethe speaks of the way colours are 'acts of light' (E, xxxvii; G, 315), ways in which Nature manifests itself to the sense of sight, as Nature manifests itself to the other senses in other ways through other senses. In all these 'still it is Nature that speaks and manifests her presence, her power, her pervading life and the vastness of her relations' (E, xxxviii; G, 315). As Goethe says, 'However manifold, complicated, and unintelligible this language [*diese Sprache*] may often seem to us, yet its elements remain ever the same' (E, xxxviii; G, 316).

These 'elements' of nature's language are all one trope or another. Nature speaks by synecdoche, for example when the part tells what is going on in the invisible and imponderable whole. Nature 'has even a secret agent [*einen Vertrauten*; more properly 'confidant, intimate friend'] in inflexible matter, in a metal, the smallest portions of which tell us what is passing in the entire mass' (E, xxxviii). In various kinds of condensation and displacement, that is, in metaphor and metonymy, as well as in synecdoche, Nature everywhere speaks through her oscillation in 'light poise and counterpoise', according to 'a greater and lesser principle, an action and resistance, a doing and suffering, an advancing and retiring, a violent and moderating power' (E, xxxviii–ix; G, 316; Eastlake leaves out in this list phrases in Goethe's German that make explicit the personification of Nature. He attributes to Nature 'ein Männliches, ein Weibliches [a manly, a womanly]' power).

Goethe's theory of colours is a theory of tropes, of turnings and substitutions. It is not idly that figures of speech have traditionally been spoken of as 'colours of rhetoric'. Real colours out there among other 'phenomena' (*Erscheinungen*) (E, xxxix; G, 316) are figures for ungraspable Nature, not her direct manifestation. The colours of Nature are as much tropes as any verbal figure of speech in a poem is. Or rather, Goethe's theory of colours is part of a universal theory of tropes whereby we interpret the language of Nature as she speaks in different ways to different senses: 'And thus as we descend the scale of being, Nature speaks to other senses – to known, misunderstood, and unknown senses: so speaks she to herself and to us in a thousand modes [*Erscheinungen*]' (E, xxxviii; G, 315). The word *Erscheinungen* here, which East-lake somewhat misleadingly translates as 'modes', is a close relative of the key term in Hegel's definition, already twice cited, of the Beautiful as the sensible appearance ('Scheinen') of the Idea.

I have said that catachresis is one of the tropes implied in Goethe's theory of colours. It would be better to say that all these tropes are forms of catachresis. All are so many figurative emblems for ungraspable Nature. Each of the other figures is a species of catachresis, since there is no literal language for Nature, only the panoply of figures for it. As Goethe says, 'the observers of Nature have seen everywhere in Nature, approached by whatever sense, "poise and counterpoise", an advancing and retiring'. Their problem has been 'to represent such a relation in terms [*zu bezeichnen*]' (E, xxxix; G, 316; Eastlake's translation is a little odd here: *bezeichnen* means 'put a mark on, indicate, designate, name'). The relation can only be expressed figuratively, in metaphor, synecdoche, metonymy, personification, in all those exchanges, substitutions, displacements making up the spectrum of the colours of rhetoric. Therefore, says Goethe, 'a symbolical language [*eine Sprache, eine Symbolik*] has arisen which, from its close analogy, may be employed as equivalent [*als Gleichnis*] to a direct and appropriate terminology' (E, xxxix; G, 316). This language is not a direct and appropriate terminology, an adequate literal language, since no such language exists or is possible. It is a tropological substitute for that, a *Gleichnis*, a system of catachreses.

Goethe's aim, as he says, is to apply and expand this 'symbolical language' to the realm of colours and thereby to develop an appropriate theory for this topic. The colours themselves are already tropes, signs revealing ungraspable

Nature indirectly, in the only way she can be made manifest, brought to light, illustrated. The language of theory is a system of tropes about those tropes:

> To apply these universal designations, this language of Nature to the subject we have undertaken; to enrich and amplify this language by means of the theory of colours and the variety of their phenomena [*Erscheinungen*], and thus facilitate the communication of higher theoretical views, was the principle aim of the present treatise (E, xxxix-xl; G, 316).

Personification, as I have said, must be included among the tropes in a theory of colours. This might seem no more than a bow on my part in the direction of Nietzsche. Nietzsche, it will be remembered, in 'On Truth and Lie in a Non-Moral Sense', includes personification along with metaphor and metonymy in the 'mobile army' of tropes making up human language and human experience. But readers of Goethe's *Die Wahlverwandtschaften* (translated as *Elective Affinities*) will know the close connection there between the terminology for personal relations and the terminology for chemical relations of earths and minerals. The title of the novel names both at once. If it borrows a word from chemistry – *Wahlverwandtschaften* – to define amatory relations, love both inside and outside marriage, *Zur Farbenlehre* borrows, necessarily, language from human relations to define the realm of colours. Goethe, for example, ascribes, in prosopopoeia, 'an action and resistance, a doing and suffering' to the manifestations of hidden Nature, as though they were actors on some tragic stage, or he speaks of Nature as a 'she', at least in the translation: 'She is nowhere dead nor silent [*ist sie nirgends tot noch stumm*]' (E, xxxviii; G, 315). We cannot *not* see Nature and all her manifestations as in one way or another a person or a dramatic action of persons engaged in some kind of give and take, battle and lovemaking at once.

Irony, finally, appears in Goethe's extraordinary definition of what he means by theory. The word *theory*, it will be remembered, has the same root as the word *theatre*. Both words involve seeing, a 'view'. What is abstract about theory is in fact what is abstract about seeing, or about illustration, as Goethe's contemporary Hegel affirmed in that strange little essay of 1806, 'Who Thinks Abstractly?'. Any illustration for the purpose of understanding the invisible idea or ungraspable Nature by way of something that may be seen is an abstraction from the whole. It is an inadequate symbol, a catachresis. All theory or making visible by way of illustration should undercut itself, suspend itself, reveal its own inadequacy in the moment of putting itself forward. The name for this self-suspension or self-negation is 'irony'. Theory, illustration, abstraction, reflection as light turned on an object and as an act of mental consideration, the aesthetic, catachresis and irony – all, surprisingly, are names for the same mode of putting forward signs. 'Every act of seeing', says Goethe,

> leads to consideration, consideration to reflection, reflection to combination, and thus it may be said that in every attentive look on Nature we already theorise [*theoretisieren*]. But in order to guard against the possible abuse of this abstract view, in order that the practical deductions we look to should be really useful, we should theorise without forgetting that we are doing so, we should theorise with mental self-possession [*mit Bewußtsein, mit Selbstkenntnis, mit Freiheit*], and, to use a bold word, with irony' (E, xl-xli; G, 317).

In this quite extraordinary formulation, theorizing must be suspended with the parabasis of irony. Theory must be ironized if what is abstract about it, that is, the way it is drawn away tropologically from the whole it represents, is not to be taken, falsely, as literal rather than figurative.

It is now possible to see what is, somewhat obscurely, at stake in Goethe's polemic against Newton in *Zur Farbenlehre*. The opposition of Goethe to Newton is a conflict of two theories of the sign or of symbolism. Newtonian colour, made by the prismatic breaking of light, would be part of the light from which it comes. This would correspond to a notion of symbol in the Coleridgean sense. Such a symbol is an actual part of the whole to which it corresponds, genuinely similar to it, participating in it, and therefore giving direct access to it, as all Nature, for Coleridge, speaks by symbolic analogy for God as Logos, the Logos as Word and light at once. Goethe's material colours, on the other hand, correspond to an allegorical notion of the sign as catachresis, as the always ironically inadequate exterior manifestation of something hidden, profound and ungraspable. Goethe must therefore affirm that colours are intrinsic aspects of material objects, not just reflected on them by aerial light.

A speech by Mephistopheles in the study scene in part One of Goethe's *Faust* is a diabolic version of Goethe's colour theory, while the great opening section of *Faust*, part Two, the sunrise scene, is a dramatization of this anti-Newtonian view, this view of Nature as a polemical dialectic between aerial colours and material colours. Mephistopheles claims that night is the mother of light and supports this by the assertion that light and colour are not independent but come from bodies:

> I am but part of a part that was the whole at first,
> Part of the dark which bore itself the light,
> That supercilious light which lately durst
> Dispute her ancient rank and realm to Mother Night;
> And yet to no avail, for strive as it may,
> It cleaves in bondage to corporeal clay.
> It streams from bodies, bodies it lends sheen
> [*Von Körpern strömt's, die Körper macht es schön*] . . .
> (*Faust*, I, 1349–55)[105]

The streaming of light from bodies is a defiant rejection of the assumption that light is an independent originating power in the universe, father of all, the paternal Logos himself. The beautifying of objects when they are illuminated is the release from them of colours that are intrinsic to them. These colours make them sensible appearances of the 'idea', that obscure chthonian whole, dark and light together, of which each independent object is only a part. The sun too is a part that every day momentarily detaches itself from the abyss of night and becomes the most august example of the sensible shining of the Idea.

The scene in part Two of *Faust* matches a Turner sunrise in presenting the violence of the matutinal appearance of light. 'A stupendous clangor [*Ungeheures Getöse*]', says the stage direction, 'proclaims the approach of the sun'. Deafening sound here speaks for dazzling light in a synesthetic displacement that is another evidence that Nature can only be signified in trope. Faust's speech ends the scene with the claim that each person and object in Nature has life and colour not by reflection of the sun's light, but by refraction of colours that are in each case intrinsic to that person or object: 'Life is not Life, but the refracted color' [*Am farbigen Abglanz haben wir das Leben*] (*Faust*, II, 4727; E, p.121; G, p. 149; the translation here is a little loose. A more literal version would say: 'We have life from coloured refraction').

RETURN TO TURNER

I return, after this detour into Goethe, to Turner's two paintings in illustration of Goethe. Turner, I am arguing, understood Goethe very well. His Goethe paintings, along with all his other paintings of the rising or setting of the sun, enact in one way or another, on the canvas, something like the Goethean conflict of aerial colour and material colour. They enact it in Turner's attempt to produce on canvas with material pigments something that will not only represent Nature but substitute an optical effect for the aerial colours of Nature, as, for example, his *Regulus* presents a second sun that blinds the eye, not just a harmless mediated picture of the sun. Turner's 'Goethe paintings' too, like *Zur Farbenlehre*, are based on a theory of signs, in this case the painted shapes on canvas, as catachresis, as irony, as personification, as one form or another of trope. What, for example, is *The Angel Standing in the Sun* (illus. 41) but a double representation of the inherence of personification in any perception of Nature, even perception of the sovereign source of light itself? Even the blazing sun can only be seen as inhabited by a man or with a human figure superimposed on it, just as *Ulysses Deriding Polyphemus* (illus. 32) has a faintly discernible line drawing of the chariot and horses of Apollo,[106] to which Goethe also refers in Ariel's song in the sunrise scene in *Faust*. I quote the German to indicate Goethe's onomatopoeia:

Felsentore knarren rasselnd,
Phöbus' Räder rollen prasselnd,
Welch Getöse bringt das Licht![107]

Granite portals groan and clatter,
Wheels of Phoebus roll and spatter,
What great din the dawning brings![108]

In a similar way, all those mythological, historical and literary narratives – the stories of Dido, Regulus, Ulysses and

Polyphemus and so on – are superimposed, in Turner's paintings, on what initially may have been no more than what Finberg, a cataloguer of the twenty thousand or so drawings in the Turner Bequest, called 'Colour Beginnings'. They impose personages or a story on what, at another level, are only figurative relationships of strands and splotches of material colour. The angel standing in the sun is an indication that man can only see Nature by projecting his own form on it in prosopopoeia. At the same time, by way of the allusion already noted in Ruskin's identification of Turner with the Angel of the Apocalypse, the angel standing in the sun is Turner's boldest and most explicit claim that if, as he said, 'the sun is God',[109] Turner himself is also the sun or the double of the sun. Turner possesses a kingly and godlike creativity deriving from mastery over colour and light.

Paulson has associated Turner's name with the whirling vortex of colours swirling around the sun in his paintings. These paintings are a punning self-portrait and hyperbolic Promethean or Apollonian boast of the painter's heliotropic power as turner. 'Turner' also can be taken to mean troper, turner of figures, one after the other, each a new figure of the sun and of what the sun brings to light. The word 'turner', like the word *pierre* in French, is both a proper name, that is, the designator of a unique individual, and at the same time a common noun. 'Turner' names all the things of any sort that turn other things or are themselves turning.

The double bind of Turner as troper and the story told in different ways by all his paintings of the sun is the following: If Turner's paintings are only tropes of the sun's trajectory, mock or imitation suns, then he plays the role of the sun only in figure. He accomplishes nothing in reality, only in the unreal world of trope. Hence he is a tame Prometheus or Polyphemus, an object of derision to the real sun. He is darkened and darkener, not an enlightener but a bringer of 'minotony [sic], discord, and mud'. He is blinded and unmanned. On the other hand, the real sun is only an *Abglanz*, in Goethe's term, of ungraspable Nature, a trope. In making a mock sun in pigment, Turner is doing what the real sun does. Therefore he is condemnable, subject to the same punishment accorded the sun every day when it is swallowed up in the depths. The two forms of light, aerial colour and material colour, are in fact the same, destined to suffer the same fate.

144

The real sun, along with any sun made of pigment, is only a figure for what remains permanently invisible.

On the one hand, to make a mock sun is the highest artistic act. It is the act of illustration, of bringing to light, the aesthetic act *par excellence*: to make a 'sinnliche Scheinen der Idee'. On the other hand, to make a mock sun is the most dangerous act of aesthetic sacrilege. The illustration is never the real sun, maker of aerial colour, only an image of it. The image of the sun is therefore a darkening, as all material pigment tends toward mud. Such an act of desecration, challenging the sun to its face, is punished by blinding, or by effacement, as the sun has taken revenge on so many of Turner's paintings by deteriorating their pigments and cracking or flaking their surfaces.[110]

The sun's defiant imitator is even punished by beheading, another displaced form of emasculation. The latter motif appears in one of the illustrative anecdotes in Hegel's essay 'Who Thinks Abstractly?' Hegel tells another version of the story I have found told by Ruskin, by Heidegger, by Holbein, by Phiz, by Goethe and by Turner. Hegel's illustrative anecdote informs us that, with yet another turn of the screw, the challenger of the sun who is punished for his temerity becomes then truly sunlike, heroic, worthy of the sun by becoming an elucidation of the sun's journey. The beheaded murderer is a victim of our tendency to darken the real by thinking abstractly, in this case by categorizing him as simply a murderer. This abstraction is brought to life again for Hegel by 'a common old woman' who sees in the sun-illumined murderer's head an exposure of the solar law of disappearance and return:

> I once heard a common old woman . . . kill the abstraction of the murderer and bring him to life for honor. The severed head had been placed on a scaffold, and the sun was shining. How beautifully, she said, the sun of God's grace shines on Binder's head! [*wie doch so schön, sagte sie, Gottes Gnadensonne* Binders *Haupt beglänzt*] – Why you are not worthy of having the sun shine on you, one says to a rascal with whom one is angry. This woman saw that the murderer's head was struck by the sunshine and thus was still worthy of it.[111]

Of all this ironically doubled and redoubled story of the double of the sun, Turner's The 'Sun of Venice' Going to Sea (illus. 43) will serve as a final illustration. It illustrates also the relation of graphic to verbal in all those works of art where the two media work together or at cross-purposes. The sail of the fishing-boat in Turner's painting has on it a painted sun. The real sun is represented at a double remove on Turner's canvas in that place where Turner usually paints his image of the sun. Turner has painted on his canvas the painted sun on the canvas of the sail. Behind the nearest boat, the Sun of Venice itself, there is another boat, as if to put the motif of doubling before the spectator's eyes. Behind the two boats, off to the left, may be faintly discerned the Doge's Palace, the Campanile and St Mark's, with, according to Ruskin, the tower of San Giorgio Maggiore on the far left.[112] The ships are going south or south-eastward in the morning, out past the Isola di San Giorgio toward the Lido and the open sea, perhaps into the eye of the sun. In that central radiance the beholder of the painting may stand, or, as is more probable, the location of the sun is off to the right, that is, toward the east. This may be indicated by the path of yellow light coming from the right across the water, as well as by the faint shadow in the water to the left of the Sun of Venice. But the centrality of the spectator's position is indicated by the concentric half-circles of waves around the viewer's place in the foreground of the painting. Another faint series of waves is centred on the canvas (of the sail and of the painting) and on the dazzling, diffused white glow of light cast toward the west by the morning sun. Those waves almost seem to radiate from some second real sun hidden behind the painted sun on the canvas. The reflection of the ships on the water, though it is reflection, not shadow, appears to support that way of seeing the paintings.

The sun on the sail is a part of the painted scene there representing once more the harbour, ships and buildings of Venice, with a faint red and white striped line on the left of the sail doubling the line of the Campanile at the far left of Turner's painting proper. The painting on the sail duplicates the painting which duplicates the real scene, in a mise-en-abyme of receding representations within representations, of which the faint reflection in the water of the fishing-boat and its sail is the last in the series. Painted sun and painted Venice are doubled in reverse in the sea, where the painted sun is mirrored as a dull yellow spot in the water, as though to anticipate the swallowing up of all these suns by the sea, the real sun and all its simulacra. Or rather, as in Francis Ponge's poem 'Le soleil placé en abîme', the relation is not so much that implicitly grounded structure of representation within representation of the *mise-en-abyme*,[113] as the double bind of an oscillation between representations that are contiguous as well as one inside the other. Each both encircles or frames the other and is encircled by it, in a constant turning inside-out. Just as when verbal inscription and graphic representation are set side by side, each turns the other into a form of itself, so the effect of Turner's double, triple or quadruple representation of the sun in *The 'Sun of Venice' Going to Sea* is to affirm that whatever the real sun can do, his painting can also do. The painting encloses the real sun within itself, incorporates the play of real light within its own structure, while at the same time being encircled by that real sun and sharing its fate. The real sun is turned into another graphic–verbal sign. All its doubles in word or in picture are as much bringings to light, illustrations, as the 'real' sun itself.

The painting is ambiguous as to the location of the sun. If it is sunset, the 'real' sun is behind the painted sun, shedding that dazzling, diffused white glow over all the western sky. The painting then affirms the painter's sovereign power to replace the real sun by a painted sun of the same efficacy. If it is sunrise (as it almost certainly is), and if the boats have turned far enough toward the east, then that structure is doubled once more by another sun located where the painter stood to paint the painting and where the spectator stands to see it. Viewer and artist together become that angel standing in the sun, personification of the sun's all-creating power. If, as is more probable, the ship is still going south, the sun is off to the right, invisible beyond the edge of the canvas. If so, then the viewer, as the centre of those semicircular waves in the foreground of the painting, is, like the sun on the sail of the *Sun of Venice*, another mock sun. The spectator, like the painter, is an organizing centre of seeing and representing but not a source of light.

To have the experience of being put in the place of the sun

even in this displaced way is, however, not to experience consciousness as an encompassing, radiating source, but to experience one's self as, like the 'real' sun itself, another trope, therefore, like any trope, secondary, derived. The spectator becomes another catachresis for the ungraspable original, if original there is, of an interminable series of suns, each destined to rise and set, appear and disappear, each a sideways displacement for the others. Each englobes the others, but in its turn is englobed by each of them. In this movement the apparent centre shifts from spectator to artist, to invisible real sun off the canvas to the right, to putative 'real' sun behind the painted sun on the canvas, to reflected painted sun in the water, to the word 'Sol' on the sail, to the title inscribed beneath or beside the painting, to the verses appended to the painting by Turner in the exhibition catalogue, and then back through the series to the spectator, in a ceaseless coming and going that has no fixed source or stable standing-place. This is another example of the relation Foucault calls 'similitude' or 'simulacrum', as opposed to 'representation'. The verbal doublings of the graphic ones are incorporated in the graphic representations as more items in the series, not different from the graphic signs in function. They are certainly not endowed with power to undo the double bind or to put a stop to the back and forth movement of displacement and dis-displacement.

The portrait of the sun on Turner's canvas is doubled one last time by the verbal inscription that says 'Sol de VENEZ[I]A' followed by the faint, almost illegible, letters 'mi rai.i . . . [?]'.[114] Each person to whom I have presented these letters has had a different hypothesis about what they are and what they might mean.[115] Butlin and Joll say the letters were damaged and have been subsequently retouched, no doubt according to the retoucher's hypothesis, so it is now impossible to be sure just what Turner put on the canvas there. A colleague from the University of Zurich, Martin Heuser, has recently checked the original painting and tells me the letters are unreadable. They may from the beginning have been intentionally illegible, paintings of letters rather than real letters. These unintelligible letters, like the strange designs that seem to be letters in an unknown alphabet in those late paintings by Paul Klee mentioned earlier, are another place where graphic as image and graphic as word converge in the materiality of the sign. Just as a viewer, confronted by splotches of colour, mere blobs of paint on the canvas, struggles instinctively to see them as pictures of something or other, so a viewer struggles to read these letters and to make intelligible words out of them. When this effort fails with either kind of sign, the viewer catches a glimpse, though only a fleeting one, a glimpse that is not really a glimpse, of the materiality behind or beneath both image and word. This materiality is another name for what Goethe calls 'ungraspable Nature'. It is both catachrestically revealed and at the same time covered over in both picture and word when they are 'read', for example in seeing them as 'mi ra . . .'.

The possibility that 'mi ra . . .' may somehow mean 'darken me' is fulfilled in the verses Turner claims are from his 'Fallacies of Hope', modelled on lines in Gray's 'The Bard'. Turner included these verses in the catalogue when the painting was exhibited in 1843. The lines illustrate the painting and remove any hope we might have that the brave *Sun of Venice* is in the protection of the sun and will return safely to its home port laden with fish.

Like *Ulysses Deriding Polyphemus*, Turner's *The 'Sun of Venice' Going to Sea* has a political message. As John Dixon Hunt has remarked, there is a long tradition of the picturing of the sun on a ship's sail and of representing political power by a ship. The fate of the *Sun of Venice* is an emblem of the fall of the Venetian Empire as well as of the personal and aesthetic drama of Turner's imitation of the sun. Turner's verses confirm what the painting itself does not show, namely that the time is morning, not evening, so that the real sun is not behind the painted sun on the canvas, toward the west, but eastward, to the right of the canvas. And they bring to light, before the fact, the ship's fate:

> Fair shines the morn, and soft the zephyrs blow,
> Venezia's fisher spreads his painted sail so gay,
> Nor heeds the demon that in grim repose
> Expects his evening prey.[116]

Both graphic and verbal signs here are a bringing to light that will have their reward both in illumination and in darkening. The sun shines on both the painted sun and on the inscription that says the same thing over again. Both will vanish together when the ship is swallowed up by that demon in grim repose,

Turner's borrowed personifying name here for Goethe's Nature. In the same way Turner himself and all political sovereignty will be swallowed up, as will any spectator of the painting. In meeting this fate, text and illustration prove that they are both worthy of the sun by completing their imitation of its trajectory, and at the same time are justly obliterated for so boldly taking the name and image of the sun.

THE CRITIC AS ILLUSTRATOR

What, it might finally be asked, is the illustrative value of my illustrations? These have been intended as a means of bringing to light the issues involved in the relation of text to illustration. My illustrations are more examples of the sensible shining of the Idea. They are themselves cases of the aesthetic as Hegel defines it, concrete, sensuous, the necessary means of understanding what they illustrate. My illustrations do not, however, harmoniously combine to bring into the open some abstract idea of illustration or of the relation of graphic to verbal. Each of my illustrations means itself, like any other configuration of signs, any design in picture or in word. Illustrations are always falsifying abstractions from the ungraspable idea they never adequately bring into the open. What they bring to light they also hide. Like all illustrations, they leave the idea still out of sight, grimly reposing in the dark. They therefore bring on themselves their own punishment. Or, rather, they bring an appropriate burden of responsibility on the one who uses them to think and to do. I have used my illustrations both cognitively and performatively: cognitively to encounter the place where knowledge fails, performatively to reinsert my examples of illustration into the present historical, institutional and social context. There they will make happen whatever will happen when my words are read.

My discussion of illustration has illustrated several themes treated in the examination of cultural studies in the first part of this book. I have given an example of the way current information technologies have transformed the way we see artworks of the past. In this case our adeptness in modern multi-media forms has given a new awareness of the way multi-media works of the past generate meaning, and of the problems involved in reading such works. I have, in addition, given examples of the irreducible heterogeneity of works of art. This heterogeneity is not able to be fully accounted for by the historical, economic, technological, class and gender contexts of the works. It has something to do with constraints on the way signs work. My book itself, in its juxtaposition of heterogeneous works from different times and places, anticipates possibilities of assemblage soon to be easier with large digitized databases. One can imagine a computerized version of my essay in which each section would have a 'button' leading out to the large context of which my citations are a part and in which a much larger set of illustrations (in the sense of both pictures and texts) would be available through computer links. My essay is less a continuous argument than an array or constellation of examples, though these converge on my presiding ideas. But without an inscribed act of reading such as I have tried to provide, all the data in the biggest of databases would be little more than just that, raw data. The reading appropriates and reinscribes the data.

I have also illustrated how works of art bring something new into the world rather than reflecting something already there. This something new is constitutive rather than being either merely representational or, on the other hand, a revelation of something already there but hidden. Works of art make culture. Each work makes different the culture it enters.

I have exemplified, finally, what follows from this, namely the necessity of vigilant and detailed rhetorical reading of works of art in any medium in order to identify what is different in each. By this identification the force of the work can be passed on in a new form, through the reading, into the current cultural situation. For that new form the reader–critic must take responsibility. It cannot be blamed on the work, in spite of the critic's obligation to a faithful representation of the work. The critic must be held accountable for whatever inaugural power the reading has. This is an accountability not so much for the knowledge the reading gives as for what the reading *does* when it is re-read.

References

1 Walter Benjamin, *Illuminationen* (Frankfurt, 1969), p. 176; *Illuminations*, trans. Harry Zohn (New York, 1969), p. 242, henceforth 'G' and 'E' respectively, followed by the page reference. Several versions of this essay exist. I have used the one canonized by standard German editions and by the English translation. Philippe Lacoue-Labarthe has developed in detail the catastrophic effects of seeing the state as a work of art in a description of Nazi Germany as a case of 'national aestheticism'; see *La fiction du politique* (Paris, 1987), pp. 92–113. See also Paul de Man, 'Kant and Schiller', *Aesthetic Ideology* (University of Minnesota Press, forthcoming).

2 Jean-Joseph Goux, 'Politics and Modern Art – Heidegger's Dilemma', *diacritics*, XIX/3–4 (1989), p. 21. This issue of *diacritics* is devoted to 'Heidegger: Art and Politics'. It is of great relevance to my project in this essay. The relation between the themes of this issue of *diacritics* and the fact that it is illustrated by admirable abstract computer graphics by Sandra L. Hampson is not explicitly noted anywhere in the issue. The juxtaposition, however, is a confirmation of one of my presuppositions here: conditions of teaching and research in the humanities are being transformed by the computer and associated technologies. What the essays manifest in one way, the illustrations manifest in another.

3 See the discussion of this word *embedded* in reference 38 below.

4 I have been helped in thinking this through by Philip Leider.

5 For information about cultural studies in Australia and a lively essay about cultural studies generally, see Meaghan Morris, 'Banality in Cultural Studies', *Block 14* (1988), pp. 15–26.

6 In a letter of 5 March 1991 from JanMohamed to me.

7 David Lloyd, 'Ethnic Cultures, Minority Discourse and the State', unpublished MS, p. 8. The fact that Lloyd should have responded to my paper and I in turn to his through the exchange of computer-produced and laser-printed MSS before either of the papers has been published is an example of those changed conditions of scholarship in the humanities to be discussed later here. The humanities are in this merely catching up with the sciences, where such pre-publication exchange has been normal for the last two decades at least. Electronic mail has already made such interactions even easier and faster. It will, no doubt, come to be used more and more by humanists.

8 David Lloyd describes this eloquently: 'what is perhaps most immediately striking about the historical experience of minorities in general . . . is its determination by processes of dislocation rather than enracination. That continuing dislocation has taken many forms, materially and culturally, including the internal colonization of an already hybrid Chicana/o population and its continuing patterns of labour migration and acculturation; the enslavement and diaspora of African–Americans and their continuing economic dispersion; the genocide and displacement of Native Americans in an effort precisely to loosen their claim to "local" land rights; the immigration and

exploitation of Chinese and Filipino workers; and so forth' (op. cit., p. 13).

9 The fact that JanMohamed takes a term from computer language is significant. It is an example of the way the language of technology can be appropriated for theoretical reflection. It also raises the question of whether digital computers, almost exclusively used these days for research and writing in cultural studies, for example, may not have built into them an inclination toward binary negation rather than negation by what he calls 'analogue'. Analog computers have already shown themselves to be better for certain industrial uses where approximations rather than stark either/or oppositions are more effective. I discuss computers and cultural studies in part One's 'The Thoreau Prototype'.

10 Abdul JanMohamed, in the letter to me of 5 March 1991, characterizes this opposition as follows: 'In my book on Wright I intend to make the distinction by characterizing the first negation (practised by the dominant culture) as *digital*, which is binary, and the second negation (practised by minority cultures in various forms – from "signifyin" to the kind of violent negation that Wright explored) as *analogue*, which "negates" by invoking a whole set of differences, which can be thought of as "sublation", the "blues", or what Kojève calls "dialectical overcoming".' JanMohamed's quotation marks around 'negation', 'sublation' and 'dialectical overcoming' are important here, since the words belong to the vocabulary of 'digital negation'. They must be twisted to a new use to apply to 'negation by analogue'. JanMohamed may be alluding by word-play to analog computing. In any case, the two kinds of computers are called 'digital' and 'analog'. Digital computers express input and output only in numbers (base 2 in the case of our familiar desktops), while analog computers express input and output in a continuous 'language', like a clock with hands moving around a dial, in a way something like the differential series JanMohamed calls 'negation by analogue'.

11 See Jacques Derrida, 'La double séance', *La dissémination* (Paris, 1972), pp. 199–317; Michel Foucault, *Ceci n'est pas une pipe* (Montpellier, 1973); Gilles Deleuze, 'Platon et le simulacre', *Logique du sens* (Paris, 1969), pp. 292–307.

12 Of all these features of cultural studies the admirable essay by Abdul JanMohamed and David Lloyd, 'Toward a Theory of Minority Discourse: What is to Be Done?', their introductory essay for *The Nature and Context of Minority Discourse* (Oxford, 1990), is an excellent example, as is the whole volume, previously published as numbers 6 and 7 of *Cultural Critique*. Though no one work can characterize adequately a discourse as diverse, controversial and heterogeneous as cultural studies, I have had the essay by JanMohamed and Lloyd in mind as a salient expression of the assumptions of cultural studies. I am grateful for their comments on my discussion of cultural studies. These comments have led to revisions. A preliminary version of part One of this book, now much altered, was presented at the University of Oklahoma in October 1990 at a conference on Crossing the Disciplines: Cultural Studies in the 1990s. I was much helped by comments made on that occasion by Ronald Schleifer, Robert Con Davis and others. I am also grateful to Michael Sprinker, Donald Ross, Kathryne V. Lindberg, Wolfgang Iser, Nicholas Royle and Maud Ellmann, among others, for reading or listening to earlier versions of part One of this book and making helpful criticisms and suggestions for revision.

13 *Vorlesungen über die Aesthetik* ('Lectures on Aesthetics'), 1835, I, in

Werke in zwanzig Bänden, ed. E. Moldenhauer and K. M. Michel, XIII (Frankfurt am Main, 1970), p. 151.

14 Theodor W. Adorno's 'Über den Fetischcharakter in der Musik und die Regression des Hörens', *Zeitschrift für Sozialforschung*, VII/3 (1938), trans. as 'On the Fetish-Character in Music and the Regression of Listening', *The Essential Frankfurt School Reader*, ed. Andrew Arato and Eike Gebhardt (New York, 1978), pp. 270–99, explicitly attacks Benjamin's thesis that aura has vanished. One might be tempted to see positive possibilities in 'regressive listening', says Adorno, 'if it were something in which the "auratic" characteristics of the work of art, its illusory elements, gave way to the playful ones. However it may be with films, today's mass music shows little of such progress in disenchantment. Nothing survives in it more steadfastly than the illusion, nothing is more illusory than its reality' (p. 295). The disagreement turns on different conceptions of *aura*. For Benjamin aura is, at least initially, a quasi-religious or metaphysical shining forth. For Adorno it is mere illusion.

15 Benjamin's thought as paraphrased here should be compared to that of Martin Heidegger at the beginning of Heidegger's essay 'The Thing'. There film and television are described as bringing everything close but at the same time abolishing nearness. Heidegger's formulations are the chiasmus of Benjamin's. For Benjamin, cult value is associated with a sense of the remoteness of the cult object, while mechanical reproduction brings everything near. For Heidegger, who believes in the presence of the present, film, radio and television take away that proximity to things that allows us to see through them the revelation of Being: 'Yet the frantic abolition of all distances brings no nearness; for nearness does not consist in shortness of distance. What is least remote from us in point of distance, by virtue of its picture on film or its sound on the radio, can remain far from us. What is incalculably far from us in point of distance can be near to us. Short distance is not in itself nearness. Nor is great distance remoteness' ('Das Ding', *Vorträge und Aufsätze*, II, Pfullingen, 1967, pp. 37–55, p. 37; trans. A. Hofstadter as 'The Thing', in *Poetry, Language, Thought*, New York, 1971, pp. 165–82, p. 165).

16 *Allegories of Reading: Figural Language in Rousseau, Nietzsche, Rilke and Proust* (New Haven, 1979), pp. 79–102.

17 '. . . nouveaux procédés de pouvoir qui fonctionnent non pas au droit mais à la technique, non pas à la loi mais à la normalisation, non pas au châtiment mais au contrôle, et qui s'exercent à des niveaux et dans des formes qui débordent l'État et ses appareils', *Histoire de la sexualité, I: La Volonté de savoir* (Paris, 1976), p. 118.

18 See Walter Benjamin, *One-Way Street and Other Writings* (London, 1979), p. 62.

19 The relation between Benjamin's writing techniques and current multi-media hypertexts in computer textbases is discussed by Donald Ross and Austin Meredith in 'The Literary Scholar's Workstation: The Thoreau Prototype', unpublished grant proposal, p. 6. Donald Ross was kind enough to send me a copy of this proposal after we met at a conference on computers and scholarship in the humanities. I am grateful to him for giving me permission to quote from it. Citations from it will henceforth be indicated by page numbers in parentheses.

20 John P. Leavey Jr, *et al.*, *Glassary* (Lincoln, Nebraska, 1986).

21 For a wide-ranging discussion of the social, political and psychological effects of the new modes of electronic mediation, see Mark Poster, *The Mode of Information* (Chicago, 1990).

22 See Richard Lanham, 'The Electronic Word: Literary Study and the

Digital Revolution', *New Literary History*, xx (Winter 1989), pp. 265–90, and 'The Extraordinary Convergence: Democracy, Technology, Theory, and the University Curriculum', *South Atlantic Quarterly*, LXXXIX (Winter 1990), pp. 27–50.

23 See the brilliantly provocative book by Nicholas Royle, *Telepathy and Literature: Essays on the Reading Mind* (London, 1991). See also Jacques Derrida, 'Télépathie', *Furor*, 2 (February 1981), pp. 5–41.

24 See reference 19 above.

25 'We propose to put all the Thoreau materials on a disk, and all the source references Thoreau used on that same disk – along with maps, drawings of birds and plants, bird songs and natural noises, tintypes, newspapers, etc.' (p. 8).

26 The ambitious IRIS intiative at Brown for computerized teaching is now being much reduced and its original space allotted to a more conventional project in cultural studies. Nevertheless the new technologies potentially could transform the classroom as well as research. Media Services and the Office of Academic Computing of the University of California at Irvine demonstrated in May 1991 a prototype of 'the Technology Enhanced Classroom' (TEC). This classroom includes 'facilities for video and data projection, computer presentations, video-disk and CD-ROM technologies, as well as a stereo sound system and a campus network connection'. Some of the questions I raise here about the way uses of the computer for teaching and research may have built into them now dubious presuppositions about the ways literary texts and other cultural artefacts have meaning may be answered by George P. Landow's *Hypertext: The Convergence of Critical Theory and Technology* (Baltimore and London, 1991), not yet available to me.

27 See D. A. Miller, 'The Novel as Usual: Trollope's ''Barchester Towers'' ', *The Novel and the Police* (Berkeley, Los Angeles and London, 1988), pp. 107–45.

28 Abdul JanMohamed has made careful discriminations about this in the letter to me of 5 March 1991: 'The experience of any given dominated (i.e. ethnic or gender) group should not be privileged above that of other groups. We [David Lloyd and I] never advocate the celebration of ''ethnicity'' as such; rather, we wish to emphasize the need to examine (and celebrate) those cultural products that have emanated from subject-positions that have been marginalized and severely undervalued, which historically happen to be the subject-positions to which ethnic groups and women have been relegated.'

29 From the letter to me of 5 March 1991. See also JanMohamed and Lloyd, *The Nature and Context of Minority Discourse* (Oxford and New York, 1990), p. 9: 'The theory of minority discourse should neither fall back on ethnicity or gender as an a priori essence nor rush into inculcating some ''nonhumanist'' celebration of diversity for its own sake. Rather, ethnic or gender differences must be perceived as one of many residual cultural elements; they retain the memory of practices that have had to be (and still have to be) repressed so that the capitalist economic subject may be more efficiently produced . . . ''Becoming minor'' is not a question of essence (as the stereotype of minorities in dominant ideology would want us to believe) but a question of position: a subject-position that in the final analysis can be defined only in ''political'' terms – that is, in terms of the effects of economic exploitation, political disfranchisement, social manipulation, and ideological domination on the cultural formation of minority subjects and discourses. The project of systematically

articulating the implications of that subject-position – a project of
exploring the strengths and weaknesses, the affirmations and negations
that are inherent in that position – must be defined as the central task
of the theory of minority discourse.'

30 The phrases are from Edward W. Said's 'Representing the Colonized:
Anthropology's Interlocutors', *Critical Inquiry*, xv (Winter 1989), p. 223.
But see Henry Louis Gates Jr's comments on Said's essay in 'Critical
Fanonism', *Critical Inquiry*, xvii (Spring 1991), p. 459. Gates's essay,
in its survey of different contemporary ways of appropriating Fanon,
exemplifies the contentious and heterogeneous terrain of
present-day cultural criticism. It also exemplifies another important
feature of cultural criticism, namely the way in which some work within
it is purely theoretical, that is, the citation and discussion in a new
essay of a wide variety of previous theoretical essays. This operation is
sometimes carried on with little direct reference to any of the cultural
manifestations that are being theorized. Gates's essay cites and
discusses Edward W. Said, Albert Memmi, Homi K. Bhabha, Benita
Parry, Abdul JanMohamed, Gayatri Chakravorty Spivak, Stephen
Feuchtwang and others, but, as he says himself at the beginning of
his essay, it does not read in detail Fanon himself, much less any
specific aspects of African culture: 'What follows may be a prelude to
a reading of Fanon, but does not even begin that task itself' (p. 458).
The essay exemplifies the point made in my opening paragraph
above. The focus sometimes shifts from what is theorized to the
contentions among the theorists. This is a normal feature of a new
field that is just establishing itself. Moreover, as David Lloyd
asserts, the development of theory is essential to the political act of
contesting the dominant culture and empowering the margins. In any
case, an abundance of analyses of specific texts or other kinds of
works is also being produced by cultural studies, often as a testing
out of some theoretical formulation or challenge to it. Examples are
many of the admirably concrete readings in *The Nature and Context
of Minority Discourse*, cited above in reference 12. In this practice of
reading examples as an essential stage in the development of
theory, cultural studies are consonant with strategies of rhetorical
criticism, or so-called Deconstruction, as it is practiced by de Man
and Derrida, or, for that matter, by myself in this book. For rhetorical
criticism, theory almost always arises from the 'reading' of some
'primary' text or other cultural manifestation, for example paintings
or illustrations, and must remain rooted in that activity of reading, even
though theory and reading turn out to be asymmetrical. Each new
reading challenges and alters, or even disqualifies, initial
theoretical assumptions. Such reading, it might be argued, is likely
to be more actively engaged in history and culture than the abstract
give and take of theoretical debate, even though a 'theoretical'
statement like *The Communist Manifesto* may enter decisively into
history and change it. I have written above of the necessity for reading
to be material, active, interventionist, rather than simply thematic,
if it is to avoid blindly repeating the ideology that is being contested.
Only such a reading can be inaugural in the way I define that in the
last section of part One of this book.

31 See Benedict Anderson, *Imagined Communities: Reflections on the Origin
and Spread of Nationalism* (London and New York, 1983);
Jean-François Lyotard, 'Sensus communis', *Le Cahier du Collège
Internationale de Philosophie*, 3 (March 1987), pp. 67–87; with an English
translation by Geoffrey Bennington and Marian Hobson in *Paragraph*,
xi (1988), pp. 1–23; *The Differend: Phrases in Dispute*, trans. Georges

Van De Abbeele (Minneapolis, 1988); *Peregrinations* (New York, 1988); Jean-Luc Nancy, *La communauté désœuvrée* (Paris, 1986); Maurice Blanchot, *La communauté inavouable* (Paris, 1983); David Carroll, 'Community After Devastation: Culture, Politics, and the "Public Space" (Arendt, Lyotard, Nancy)', forthcoming.

32 Minority discourse, writes David Lloyd, 'is by no means committed . . . to the preservation of culture for its own sake. It recognizes specific values in all cultural formations, especially where these intimate the possibility of a fuller collective existence, but does so in the full recognition that under conditions of domination all cultures are "products of damage" and in need of transformation. Its project is accordingly not to preserve cultural forms but to contribute, through cultural analysis, to the securing of the maximum possible degree of self-determination in every sphere for all people, individuals or groups' (op. cit., p. 16). 'Self-determination' is, of course, a problematic term here. It requires further specifying to distinguish it from the model of the free subject in a democratic state. The latter is part of the dominant ideology of liberal capitalism that is being contested. Another example of a problematic word and of the need to twist old terms to new uses is 'empower'. The word belongs to the ideology of the dominant culture. In what sense, exactly, do cultural studies aim to 'empower' marginalized groups? How can the word and the act avoid a symmetrical reinstatement of some unjust hierarchy? The concluding section of part One here suggests an answer. Benjamin's 'The Critique of Violence', trans. E. Jephcott, *Reflections* (New York, 1979), pp. 277–300, is essential reading to help think through this problem.

33 Martin Heidegger, 'Der Ursprung des Kunstwerkes', *Holzwege* (Frankfurt, 1972), p. 64; trans. A. Hofstadter as 'The Origin of the Work of Art', *Poetry, Language, Thought* (New York, 1971), p. 77, henceforth 'G' and 'E' respectively, followed by the page reference.

34 See Drucilla Cornell, 'Time, Deconstruction, and the Challenge of Legal Positivism: The Call for Judicial Responsibility', *Yale Journal of Law & the Humanities*, II/1 (Summer 1990), pp. 267–97. And see also the brilliant chapter on Foucault, 'The "paradox" of power and knowledge (Foucault)', in Thomas Keenan's *Difficult Responsibilities: Rights of Fable*, unpublished Yale dissertation, 1990. A preliminary version of this has been published as 'The "Paradox" of Knowledge and Power: Reading Foucault on a Bias', *Political Theory*, XV/1 (February 1987), pp. 5–37. For a recognition that each national identity is by no means a single essence except in mystified ideological affirmations, but is continually making itself and is the site of a perpetual warfare among different interest groups, so that a liminal or marginal space always exists in the gap between signifier and fixed ideological signification for effective performative speech acts, even by disempowered minorities, see Homi K. Bhabha, 'DissemiNation: time, narrative, and the margins of the modern nation', *Nation and Narration: Post-structuralism and the Culture of National Identity* (New York, 1990), pp. 291–322. For a forceful critique of Bhabha's formulations in an earlier essay, 'Signs, taken for Wonders: Questions of Ambivalence and Authority under a Tree outside Delhi, May 1817', *Critical Inquiry*, XII/1 (Autumn 1985), pp. 144–65, see Benita Parry, 'Problems in Current Theories of Colonial Discourse', *Oxford Literary Review*, IX (Winter 1987), pp. 27–58.

35 For an extended analysis of this essay see Jacques Derrida, 'Force of Law: The "Mystical Foundation of Authority"', *Cardozo Law Review*, XI/5–6 (July/August 1990), pp. 919–1045.

36 See Jacques Derrida, *Memoires for Paul de Man*, trans. C. Lindsay, J. Culler and E. Cadava (New York, 1986), p. 57: 'Memory projects itself toward the future, and it constitutes the presence of the present. The "rhetoric of temporality" is the rhetoric of memory . . . Resurrection, which is always the formal element of "truth", a recurrent difference between a present and its presence, does not resuscitate a past which had been present; it engages the future.'

37 The issue of the *Cardozo Law Review* cited above in reference 35 is a good example of this.

38 Stephen Greenblatt's problematic figure for this is *embedded*: 'Social actions are themselves always embedded in systems of public signification always grasped, even by their makers, in acts of interpretation, while the words that constitute the works of literature that we discuss here are by their very nature the manifest assurance of a similar embeddedness.' As a result, the object of study is 'both the social presence to the world of the literary text and the social presence of the world in the literary text' (Greenblatt, *Renaissance Self-Fashioning*, Chicago, 1980, p. 5). The 'systems of public signification' transcend both social actions and works of literature, both of which are 'embedded' in those systems. Greenblatt's formulations have the virtue of recognizing that no sharp line can be drawn between text and context. Each has been invaded by the other or overlaps with it, in a relation that the word *embedded* hints is quasi-sexual. Greenblatt also recognizes that the text transforms and remakes the context rather than simply reflecting it or being made by it. The figure of 'embeddedness', however, is limited by suggesting, in spite of linguistic terms like 'signification', 'words' and 'works of literature', that the relation between a work of literature and the systems of public signification is physical or material, however dynamic it may be. The relation is rhetorical or figurative, not material. Any terminology that ignores this will be aberrant, according to an almost irresistible penchant for seeing sign to sign relations as thing to thing relations. If the latter can be accounted for in terms suitable for describing material systems, only a rhetorical or tropological terminology will account for the former.

39 The further development of this complex problematic of the inaugural performative as it is specifically exemplified in the work of the cultural critic must here be deferred as work for the future. I have elsewhere developed more fully the structure of this faithfulness that at the same time makes something new and through which the one who performs it is himself or herself made new while at the same time being obliged to say 'I did it. I take responsibility for it'. See my *Versions of Pygmalion* (Cambridge, Mass., 1990), especially the chapters on Kleist and on James's *What Maisie Knew*. Maisie is a salient example of someone who acts, who chooses, who does something with words that cannot be fully accounted for by her subject-position, even though that position is specified by James with dazzling specificity as necessary to gaining as much understanding as possible of the meaning of her final speech act.

40 'Sur le livré illustré', *Oeuvres complètes*, ed. Henri Mondor (Paris, 1945), p. 878.

41 Heraclitus, fr. 6, in G. S. Kirk and J. E. Raven, *The Presocratic Philosophers: A Critical History with a Selection of Texts* (Cambridge, 1966), p. 202, n. 228. The relevance of two more citations from the Presocratics will become clear as my argument progresses: 'Helios son of Hyperion descended into his golden cup, that, having passed

over Okeanos, he might come to the depths of holy, dark
night . . .' (Stesichorus, fr. 6, in Kirk and Raven, p. 14, n. 8); 'The
sun comes into being each day from little pieces of fire that are collected
. . . There are innumerable suns and moons according to regions,
sections, and zones of the earth' (Xenophanes, in Kirk and Raven,
pp. 172–3, nn. 178, 182).

42 See Michael Steig, *Dickens and Phiz* (Bloomington, Indiana, 1978);
Robert L. Patten, 'Boz, Phiz, and Pickwick in the Pound', *ELH*,
xxxvi (1969), pp. 575–91; John R. Harvey, *Victorian Novelists and Their
Illustrators* (London, 1970); Ronald Paulson, *Hogarth's Graphic
Works*, 2 vols (New Haven and London, 1970).

43 This goes back at least to Sergei Eisenstein's 'Word and Image', *Film
Sense*, trans. Jay Leyda (New York, 1947), pp. 3–68.

44 Mark Twain, *Life on the Mississippi* (New York and Scarborough,
Ontario, 1961), ch. 44, pp. 254–5.

45 This word was attached to Leonardo da Vinci by his
nineteenth-century editors. It has become a key term in current
work on the relation of word and image.

46 The relation of picture to word has recently become a distinct topic
for theoretical and historical investigation. An international
organization holds conferences to study the subject and sponsors a
journal, *Word & Image*. An important project in art practice and
theory, 'Art & Language', has been carried on since the late 1960s.
Among books in one way or another on the relation of words to
visual images, four distinguished ones are: Svetlana Alpers, *The Art
of Describing: Dutch Art in the Seventeenth Century* (Chicago, 1983);
Michael Fried, *Realism, Writing, Disfiguration: On Thomas Eakins and
Stephen Crane* (Chicago, 1987); Charles Harrison, *Essays on Art &
Language* (Oxford, 1991); W. J. T. Mitchell, *Iconology: Image, Text,
Ideology* (Chicago, 1986). Marc Shell's admirable *The Economy of Literature*
(Baltimore and London, 1978) is also partly on this topic, particularly
in relation to inscriptions on coins; see the chapter entitled 'The
Language of Character: An Introduction to a Poetics of Monetary
Inscriptions', pp. 63–88. But already in the eighteenth century the
relation between picture and word was the object of explicit
theoretical reflection, for example in Denis Diderot's 'Lettre sur les
Sourds et Muets' (1751). Diderot's essay ends with a comparison of
poetry, painting and music as ways of representing a dying
woman. For a good recent edition of the essay see Diderot, *Lettre sur
les sourds et muets*, ed. Paul Hugo Meyer (Geneva, 1965). See also
the discussion of this essay by Michael Fried in 'Toward a Supreme
Fiction', chapter Two of his *Absorption and Theatricality: Painting and
Beholder in the Age of Diderot* (Berkeley, Los Angeles and London,
1980), pp. 71–105. Diderot's analysis remains within the
assumption that the goal of all three arts, poetry, painting, music, is
the imitation of nature, though of course Diderot has a subtle and
nuanced idea of imitation.

47 *The Last Meeting of Lee and Jackson* (8½ × 6 feet) was painted in 1869 in
St Louis, Missouri, by Everett B. D. Julio (1843–79). Having passed
from Colonel John B. Richardson to Colonel James B. Sinnott, the
painting is now in the possession of Robert M. Hicklin Jr, an art
dealer in Spartanburg, South Carolina. Most reproductions have been
made from an engraving by Frederick Halpin, of New York,
executed soon after the painting was completed. See the Associated
Press article by Jay Reeves in the Lexington, Virginia, *News-Gazette*
for 31 June 1988. The death of 'Stonewall' Jackson marked a
turning-point in the Civil War. It was followed two months later

by the decisive defeat of the Confederate forces at the Battle of Gettysburg.

48 From 'The Willowdale Handcar', *Amphigorey: Fifteen Books by Edward Gorey* (New York, 1972), n.p.

49 Op. cit., in reference 46.

50 Robert Browning, 'Fra Lippo Lippi', in *The Works of Robert Browning*, ed. F. G. Kenyon, IV (New York, 1966), p. 113, ll. 295–304.

51 'Sur le livre illustré', ed. cit., p. 878.

52 Henry James, preface to *The Golden Bowl*, in *The Novels and Tales of Henry James*, reprint of the 'New York' edition, XXIII (New York, 1971), p. x.

53 This passage is cited and discussed by Ezra Pound, 'Introduction', *Ezra Pound in Italy* and in the chapter 'Illustrating Henry James' in *Alvin Langdon Coburn, Photographer: An Autobiography*, ed. H. and A. Gernsheim (London, 1966), pp. 52–60.

54 Michel Foucault, *Ceci n'est pas une pipe* (Montpellier, 1973); trans. as *This is Not a Pipe* by James Harkness (Berkeley, Los Angeles and London, 1983).

55 Op. cit., in reference 46.

56 The subtitle is *Six Lectures on Wood and Metal Engraving; with Appendix. Given Before the University of Oxford in Michaelmas Term, 1872.* The text is from *The Works of John Ruskin*, ed. E. T. Cook and Alexander Wedderburn, XXII (New York, 1906). Page numbers refer to this volume in this edition. Other citations from Ruskin will be identified by volume and page numbers in this edition.

57 I have discussed these passages in 'Ariadne's Thread: Repetition and the Narrative Line', *Critical Inquiry*, III/1 (Autumn 1976), pp. 57–77.

58 A horrifying version of the connection between engraving and writing is that story by Franz Kafka, 'In die Strafkolonie' (In the Penal Colony). In this story the condemned man's body is the writing surface. The machine of execution is a stylus that writes the sentence more and more deeply on the prisoner's body, thereby judging him and killing him with the same inscription. The prisoner learns with his body's wounds the meaning of his offence. He has finally a great 'enlightenment', but only by paying for that knowledge with his life. The insight comes at the moment of death. This story is a grotesque allegory of the 'materiality of the letter' and of the connection of writing with death explored in his own way by Ruskin.

59 Ruskin may have misunderstood Shakespeare to be referring to a morris dance rather than to the game of nine-men's morris, in which each player has nine counters, or 'men'. The game is played in a square cut in the turf. A somewhat fanciful account of a morris dance surviving as a living tradition in twentieth-century England is given in the murder scene of Ngaio Marsh's *Death of a Fool* (New York, 1963), pp. 51–61. Though the dance enacts an Oedipal ritual and turns on issues of sexual differentiation, all the performers in a morris dance are men.

60 Virgil, *Aeneid*, trans. W. F. Jackson Knight (Harmondsworth, 1959), p. 137. I have cited some phrases in Latin to indicate Virgil's play on the images of sign-reading and weaving ('signa', 'textum', 'textunt').

61 For a discussion of these and related images from a feminist perspective see Susan Gubar, ' "The Blank Page" and the Issues of Female Creativity', *Critical Inquiry*, VIII (Winter 1981), pp. 243–63.

62 See Sigmund Freud, *The Problem of Anxiety*, trans. Henry Alden Bunker (New York, 1963), p. 15.

63 The best essay on the connection of art to morality and economics in

Ruskin's thought is Marc Shell's 'John Ruskin and the Political Economy of Literature', *The Economy of Literature* (Baltimore and London, 1978), pp. 129–51.

64 I have mapped this in detail in a forthcoming essay, 'Topography'.

65 See *La Vérité en peinture* (Paris, 1978), pp. 290–436; trans. Geoff Bennington and Ian McLeod as *The Truth in Painting* (Chicago, 1987), pp. 255–382.

66 Cited in reference 33 above, henceforth 'E' and 'G', followed by the page reference.

67 See 'The Thing', in *Poetry, Language, Thought*, citation in reference 15.

68 See Philippe Lacoue-Labarthe, *La fiction du politique*, and Jean-Joseph Goux, 'Politics and Modern Art – Heidegger's Dilemma', cited above in references 1 and 2.

69 Few founders of states or even of new institutions within the state are willing to take this responsibility. Most invoke God, the rights of man, self-evident truths, a universal law, some pre-existing people, etc., as the ground for what they do. But this is an evasion. For an eloquent formulation of this situation, see Jacques Derrida, *Psyché: Inventions de l'autre* (Paris, 1987), p. 459. Derrida speaks of 'cet extraordinaire performatif par lequel une signature s'autorise elle-même à signer, en un mot se légalise de son propre chef sans le garant d'une loi préalable' (This extraordinary performative by which a signature authorizes itself to sign, in a word legalizes itself on its own responsibility without the guarantee of a pre-existing law).

70 See my discussion of this at the end of part One.

71 In the essay cited in reference 2.

72 Quoted by Lacoue-Labarthe, op. cit., p. 167, trans. Michele Sharp, and cited in the essay by Jean-Joseph Goux cited in reference 2 above.

73 Ibid.

74 See Jacques Derrida's discussion of 'trait' and 'retrait' in 'Le retrait de la métaphore', *Psyché: Inventions de l'autre* (Paris, 1987), pp. 63–93.

75 *The Eagle's Nest: Ten Lectures on the Relation of Natural Science to Art, Given Before the University of Oxford in Lent Term, 1872*, in *Works*, xxii, p. 198.

76 See reference 15 above.

77 I have here encountered through my own trajectory that 'insignificance' and 'divisibility' of the letter Jacques Derrida has approached from a different direction in, among other rendezvous, 'Mes chances: Au rendez-vous de quelques stéréophonies épicuriennes', translated by Irene Harvey and Avital Ronell as 'My Chances/*Mes Chances*: A Rendezvous with some Epicurean Stereophonies', *Taking Chances: Derrida, Psychoanalysis, and Literature* (Baltimore and London, 1984), p. 16: 'The paradox here is the following (I must state it in its broadest generality): to be a mark and to mark its marking effect, a mark must be capable of being *identified*, recognized as the same, being precisely *re-markable* from one context to another. It must be capable of being repeated, re-marked in its essential trait as the same. This accounts for the apparent solidity of its structure, of its type, its *stereotypy*. It is this that leads us here to speak of the atom, since one associates indestructibility with indivisibility. But more precisely, it is not simple [*Mais justement ce n'est pas simple*] since the identity of a mark is also its difference and its differential relation, varying each time according to context, to the network of other marks. The ideal iterability that forms the structure of all marks is that which undoubtedly allows them to be released from any context, to be freed from all determined bonds to its origin, its meaning, or its referent, to emigrate in order to play elsewhere, in whole or in part [*en totalité ou en partie*] another role. I

say "in whole or in part" because by means of this essential
insignificance [*insignifiance essentielle*] the ideality or ideal identity of
each mark (which is only a differential function without an
ontological basis) can continue to divide itself and to give rise to the
proliferation of other ideal identities. This iterability is thus that
which allows a mark to be used more than once. It is more than one.
It multiplies and divides itself internally. This imprints the capacity
for diversion within its very movement. In the destination
(*Bestimmung*) there is thus a principle of indetermination, chance,
luck, or of destinerring [*destinerrance*]. There is no assured destination
precisely because of the mark and the proper name; in other words,
because of this insignificance.' (The interpolated phrases are cited
from a manuscript of the original French version of the essay.)

78 See reference 42 above. See also Albert Johannsen, *Phiz: Illustrations
from the Novels of Charles Dickens* (Chicago, 1956), for a detailed and
authoritative account of the way Phiz's etchings for Dickens's novels
were made and of the variations from one steel to another as duplicates
were prepared or old ones reworked. On the etchings for *The Pickwick
Papers* Johannsen says: 'At first, on account of the wearing-down of the
steel plates upon which the designs were etched and later to the need
for quicker printing of the text, duplicate steels were made, in most
cases following the originals very closely but in some cases departing
radically from them. Apparently, a proof was pulled from the first
plate and transferred to the wax of the second, and then traced either
by Browne himself or by his assistant Robert Young, or later by
some other assistant. Besides this duplication of plates, there was
another cause for slight variations in the prints, for, as the plates
wore down, they were repeatedly touched up and strengthened by
crosshatching or recutting' (p. 1).

79 Steven Marcus, 'Language into Structure: Pickwick Revisited',
Daedalus, CI (1972), pp. 183–202.

80 Preface to the 'Charles Dickens Edition', 1867, in Charles Dickens,
The Posthumous Papers of the Pickwick Club, ed. Robert L. Patten
(Harmondsworth, 1972), p. 50.

81 Preface to *The Golden Bowl*, ed. cit., p. ix.

82 See Patten, op. cit., p. 582.

83 Steig, op. cit., p. 26.

84 As Evan Henerson has reminded me.

85 The iconography of this plate has been abundantly interpreted by
Patten and Steig.

86 Wallace Stevens, 'Notes Toward a Supreme Fiction', *Collected Poems*
(New York, 1954), p. 380.

87 *Images of Romanticism: Verbal and Visual Affinities*, ed. Karl Kroeber and
William Walling (New Haven and London, 1978), pp. 167–88; reprinted
in Ronald Paulson, *Literary Landscape: Turner and Constable* (New
Haven and London, 1982), pp. 63–103. I am also indebted to
comments made on oral presentations of this section on Turner by
Andrew Wilton, Ronald Paulson, Stephen Bann, Max Nänny,
Martin Heuser, W. J. T. Mitchell, James Heffernan and Terrence
Diggory.

88 Here is Robert Fitzgerald's translation of the passage:

> Now, by the Gods, I drove my big hand spike
> deep in the embers, charring it again,
> and cheered my men along with battle talk
> to keep their courage up: no quitting now.
> The pike of olive, green though it had been,
> reddened and glowed as if about to catch.

I drew it from the coals and my four fellows
gave me a hand, lugging it near the Kyklops
as more than natural force nerved them; straight
forward they sprinted, lifted it, and rammed it
deep in his crater eye, and I leaned on it
turning it as a shipwright turns a drill
in planking, having men below to swing
the two-handled strap that spins it in the groove.
So with our brand we bored that great eye socket
while blood ran out around the red hot bar.
Eyelid and lash were seared; the pierced ball
hissed broiling, and the roots popped.
                                    In a smithy
one sees a white-hot axehead or an adze
plunged and wrung in a cold tub, screaching steam –
the way they make soft iron hale and hard –:
just so that eyeball hissed around the spike.

(*The Odyssey*, trans. Robert Fitzgerald [Garden City, New York, 1963], IX, 11. 406–28, p. 156.)

89 See Nietzsche's appropriation of this in section 344 of *The Gay Science*: 'For you only have to ask yourself carefully, "Why do you not want to deceive?" especially if it should seem [*den Anschein haben sollte*] – and it does seem! – as if life aimed at semblance [*Anschein*], meaning error, deception, simulation, delusion, self-delusion, and when the great sweep of life has always shown itself to be on the side of the most unscrupulous *polytropoi* [*der unbedenklichsten πολύτροποι*]' (trans. Walter Kaufmann, New York, 1974 p. 282); Friedrich Nietzsche, *Die fröliche Wissenschaft*, in *Werke in Drei Bänden*, ed. Karl Schlecta, II (Munich, 1966), pp. 207–8.

90 Ann Arbor, Michigan: University Microfilms, 1972.

91 This description is by the painter Sir John Gilbert (1817–98). It is cited from Lionel Cust, 'The Portraits of J.M.W. Turner', *Magazine of Art* (1895), pp. 248–9, in Martin Butlin and Evelyn Joll, *The Paintings of J. M. W. Turner* (New Haven and London, 1977), I, p. 156. Ruskin disapproved of this painting, which he calls *Regulus Leaving Rome*. Ruskin saw it as a 'wicked relapse into the old rivalry with Claude' (*Works*, XIII, p. 151).

92 *Literary Gazette*, 4 February 1837, cited in Butlin and Joll, I, p. 156.

93 *Spectator*, 11 February 1837, cited in Butlin and Joll, I, p. 157.

94 See Ruskin's comment on this in *Modern Painters*, I, *Works*, III, 290: 'And it is indeed by this that the works of Turner are peculiarly distinguished from those of all other colourists, by the dazzling intensity, namely, of the light which he sheds through every hue, and which, far more than their brilliant colour, is the real source of their overpowering effect upon the eye, an effect so *reasonably* made the subject of perpetual animadversion; as if the sun which they represent were quite a quiet, and subdued, and gentle, and manageable luminary, and never dazzled anybody, under any circumstances whatsoever. I am fond of standing by a bright Turner in the Academy, to listen to the unintentional compliments of the crowd – "What a glaring thing!" "I declare I can't look at it!" "Don't it hurt your eyes?" – expressed as if they were in the constant habit of looking the sun full in the face, with the most perfect comfort and entire facility of vision.'

95 Andrew Wilton, *J.M.W. Turner: His Art and Life* (New York, 1979), pp. 220–1.

96 John Gage, *Colour in Turner: Poetry and Truth* (New York, 1969), p. 143.

97 See Horace, *Odes*, III, 5: 'He is said to have put away from him, as one whose rights were lost, the lips of his chaste wife, and his little children, and to have sternly fixed upon the ground his manly face [*et virilem / torvus humi posuisse vultum*]; until by his influence he made resolute the wavering senators with counsel given at no other time, and amid his sorrowing friends hastened away, an illustrious exile [*interque maerentis amicos / egregius properaret exsul*].
'And still he knew what the barbarian tormentor was preparing for him; he put aside his kinsmen who fain would stop him, and the people who sought to delay his return, just as if he were leaving his clients' tedious business when a suit had been decided, speeding to the fields of Venafrum, or to Tarentum the Spartan town' (*The Works of Horace*, trans. James Lonsdale and Samuel Lee, London, 1874, p. 59).

98 Many other paintings by Turner have a self-referential dimension, for example *Snow Storm – Steam-Boat off a Harbour's Mouth making Signals in Shallow Water, and going by the Lead. The Author was in this Storm on the Night the Ariel left Harwich* (exh. 1842). In order to prepare for this painting Turner had himself, like Ulysses, tied to the mast of the ship, so he could not lose his courage, though he feared the ship would be sunk. See Butlin and Joll, I, p. 224.

99 For a good recent essay on this, in connection with Goethe's *Die Wahlverwandtschaften*, see Claudia J. Brodsky, 'The Coloring of Relations: "Die Wahlverwandtschaften" as "Farbenlehre" ', *The Imposition of Form* (Princeton, N.J., 1987), pp. 88–138.

100 Notably Laurence Gowing, *Turner*, p. 5, and James A. W. Heffernan, 'The English Romantic Perception of Color', *Images of Romanticism* (New Haven, 1978), p. 143.

101 See, in addition to the works of Gowing and Heffernan cited above, Jack Lindsay, *J. M. W. Turner: His Life and Work* (London and Greenwich, Conn., 1966), p. 211. For additional scholarship on Turner's theory of colour, see John Gage, op. cit., and Gerald Finley, 'Turner: An Early Experiment with Colour Theory', *Journal of the Warburg and Courtauld Institutes*, XXX (1967), 357–66.

102 Cited by Heffernan, pp. 147–52.

103 J. W. von Goethe, *Zur Farbenlehre*, in *Werke*, XIII (Hamburg, 1962), pp. 321–2; *The Theory of Colour*, trans. Charles Lock Eastlake (Cambridge, Mass., 1970), pp. xlviii–ix. Originally published in 1840, this was the translation Turner read. Eastlake was a Royal Academy friend of his. See Graham Reynolds, *Turner* (New York and London, 1969). Further citations from works by Goethe will be from this edition and this translation, identified as G or E, followed by page numbers and volume numbers where appropriate.

104 This word is used in maxims 297 and 718 (G, XII, 406, 467): 'The further back one goes in experience [*Erfahrung*], the closer one comes to the ungraspable [*Unerforschlichen*]; the more one knows how to make use of experience, the more one sees that the ungraspable has no practical use . . . The most beautiful luck of the thinking man is to have grasped the graspable [*das Erforschliche erforscht*] and to quietly honor the ungraspable [*Unerforschliche*].' These maxims are cited by C. Brodsky, op. cit., pp. 106, 107.

105 J. W. von Goethe, *Faust: Eine Tragödie* in G, III, 47; trans. as *Faust: A Tragedy* by Walter Arndt, ed. Cyrus Hamlin (New York, 1976), p. 33.

106 As Ruskin observes, while the horses of Apollo in this painting 'are drawn in fiery outline, leaping up into the sky and shaking their crests out into flashes of scarlet cloud', Apollo is not represented: 'The god

himself is formless, he *is* the sun' (*Notes on the Turner Gallery at Marlborough House* [1857], *Works*, XIII, p. 137).

107 J. W. von Goethe, *Faust: Der Tragödie Zweiter Teil, Goethes Werke, Dramen Band*, III, p. 147, ll. 4669–71.

108 Arndt trans., ed. cit., p. 119.

109 Quoted in Paulson, op. cit., p. 83.

110 Ruskin eloquently describes this prompt solar retribution in a number of passages, one apropos of *The 'Sun of Venice' Going to Sea*, my final example of Turner's illustrations of the sun. See *Works*, III, p. 249: 'No *picture* of Turner's is seen in perfection a month after it is painted. The Walhalla cracked before it had been eight days in the Academy rooms; the vermilions frequently lose lustre long before the Exhibition is over; and when all the colors begin to get hard a year or two after the picture is painted, a painful deadness and opacity comes over them, the whites especially becoming lifeless, and many of the warmer passages settling into a hard valueless brown, even if the paint remains perfectly firm, which is far from being always the case'; of *The 'Sun of Venice'*, in 1856 Ruskin wrote: 'The sea in this picture was once exquisitely beautiful: it is not very severely injured, but it has lost much of its transparency in the green ripples. The sky was little more than flake white laid with the pallet-knife; it has got darker, and spotted, destroying the relief of the sails' (*Works*, XIII, p. 164).

111 G. W. F. Hegel, 'Who Thinks Abstractly?' in *Hegel: Texts and Commentary: Hegel's Preface to his System in a new Translation with Commentary on the Facing Pages, and "Who Thinks Abstractly?"*, trans. and ed. Walter Kaufmann (Notre Dame, Indiana, 1977), p. 117; G. W. F. Hegel, *Werke in zwanzig Bänden*, II (Frankfurt am Main, 1970), p. 579.

112 Ruskin, *Works*, XIII, p. 164. The painting was one of Ruskin's favourites, especially admired for its representation of the fishing-boat and for its painting of the sea's surface. The painting is described or praised in three places in his work, along with other passing references: twice in *Modern Painters*, I, in *Works*, III, pp. 250–1, 545–6, and later, in 1857, in *Notes on the Turner Gallery*, in *Works*, XIII, pp. 163–4. In the latter he wrote: 'The marvelous brilliancy of the arrangement of colour in this picture renders it, to my mind, one of Turner's leading works in oil' (XIII, p. 164). Ruskin was even expelled from the Royal Academy in 1843 for attempting to make pencil sketches of it (XIII, p. 163). Of the fishing-boat Ruskin comments: 'The reader, if he has not been at Venice, ought to be made aware that the Venetian fishing-boats, almost without exception, carry canvas painted with bright colors; the favorite design for the centre being either a cross or a large sun with many rays, the favorite colors being red, orange, and black, blue occurring occasionally. The radiance of these sails . . . under sunlight is beyond all painting . . .' (III, p. 545).

113 Compare Jacques Derrida's 'Restitutions', *La Vérité en peinture* (Paris, 1978), p. 391; trans. in *The Truth in Painting*, by Geoff Bennington and Ian McLeod (Chicago and London, 1987), p. 342, apropos of Van Gogh's shoes:

> – No, no, no, it says nothing of the sort, it gives nothing to be understood, especially not, yet again, that *mise-en-abyme* of painting in painting which has been clearly shown still to tend toward such a restituting saturation, such a representative readequation. No, no.

114 This is the reading of Butlin and Joll, I, p. 227. To my eye the letters look more like 'mi ragi . . .'.
115 Ronald Paulson suggests they might stand for 'mi raggia' (shine on me) or might stand for 'mi rabbine' (darken me). *Mirare* in Italian means 'to look at' or 'wonder at', another possibility, if the 'g' is the retoucher's addition. Barbara Spackman has suggested the words might be 'mi cari' (my beloved ones), though that hardly makes sense in the context.
116 Butlin and Joll, p. 228. Here are the lines (71–6) from Gray's 'The Bard':

> Fair laughs the Morn, and soft the Zephyr blows
> While proudly riding o'er the azure realm
> In gallant trim the gilded vessel goes,
> YOUTH at the prow and PLEASURE at the helm;
> Regardless of the sweeping whirlwind's sway,
> That hush'd in grim repose, expects its evening prey.

Coleridge, in his *Biographia Literaria*, asserts that Gray's source is *The Merchant of Venice*, presumably II, vi, 14–19:

> How like a younger or a prodigal
> The scarfèd bark puts from her native bay,
> Hugged and embracèd by the strumpet wind!
> How like the prodigal doth she return,
> With overweathered ribs and ragged sails,
> Lean, rent, and beggared by the strumpet wind!

Coleridge comments: 'I preferred the original [in Shakespeare] on the ground that in the imitation it depended wholly in the compositor's putting, or not putting, a *small Capital*, . . . whether the words should be personifications, or mere abstracts' (*Biographia Literaria*: I, in *The Collected Works of Samuel Taylor Coleridge*, ed. James Engell and W. Jackson Bate, Princeton, 1983, p. 20).

According to Ruskin, Turner 'wanted afterwards to make the first lines of this legend rhyme with each other; and to read: "Fair shines the moon, the Zephyr [west wind] blows a gale; / Venetia's fisher spreads his painted sail"' (Ruskin, ed. cit., XIII, p. 164). The replacement of sun by moon would certainly make nonsense of my reading (though I might see the moon as another displacement of the sun), as would any suggestion that the wind swelling those sails is coming from the west, against all topographical reality. I can only hope that the changes were intended to lead the viewer astray and to demonstrate the 'fallacies of hope' in any critic who has the temerity to challenge Turner as sun-painter to his face by trying to make a definitive reading of this painting. The interpreter's job is not made easier by the fact that Turner frequently rearranged topographical details for his own compositional purposes.